GLOBAL YOGA

AN ART OF BALANCING

Yoga - Renaissance

Swami Nigamanand Saraswati

Old order changeth, yielding place to new.
God fulfills Himself in many ways,
Lest one good custom should corrupt the world.

Morte D' Arthur
Lord Alfred Tennyson

BOOKS FOR ALL
DELHI

First Published 2013

ISBN 10: 81-7286-302-4
ISBN 13: 978-81-7386-302-8

Published by
BOOKS FOR ALL
A-6, 2nd Floor, Nimri Commercial Centre,
Ashok Vihar Phase-4, Delhi 110052 (INDIA)
Ph.: +91.11.27302453 *Fax.:* +91.11.47061936
website: LPPindia.com *e-mail:* info@LPPindia.com

Books For All
is one of the imprints of
Low Price Publications

Typesetting and Designing
Amar Creations

Printed by
D.K. Fine Art Press (P) Ltd., Delhi

PRINTED IN INDIA

DEDICATED
TO
My Yoga friend

Dr. Bhagchand Brahmecha
M.Sc., Ph.D., Physics
Founder of Nachiketa Bhalagram Pune-33

- The author

About This Book

I have completed the incomplete theory of general exercises and Yoga practices. These practices keep us healthy and cheerful even in the old age. Exercises if balanced result in spiritual growth and Yoga if unbalanced is no more than general exercises.

Life is less a thing, more a thought. Thoughts are our inner being. We cannot tolerate any attack upon our thoughts as upon our body. If the thought is true and beneficial accept it. It will give you a new life. If not, keep it under consideration. It may appeal to you in future.

Publication of this book is an important event in my life and history of Yoga. This book is the cream of my lifelong meditations and experiences. This book is more a divine revelation than a human achievement. My aim is ...

Enjoy the effort if aim is good,

To the result, pay not heed.

You may not be understood,

But blessed is your deed.

- *The author*

Invocation

Hail! Celestial light,
Empowered by Thy Grace,
I could face the trade-winds
And the ways of the world;
To find the Truth,
Dared to sip, The Elixir of Life
In the Poisonous Sea of duality.
O! Holy Spirit!
Raise me, from Humanity to Divinity.

INDEX

PART I - Physical Balance

APPENDIX

1. NEED FOR BALANCE

Law of nature is that of balance in the sphere of dualities and changes. As compared to animals, man is given freedom by nature. He misuses it. Due to ambition, he goes to the extreme, if successful, he becomes haughty, egoist and greedy. Failure creates tension, anger, violence and inferiority complex. Tension imbalances the breath and the body. So there is need for balance.

Hatha Yoga declares by lotus posture and cross breathing, the need for balance of the *Ida* and *Pingala* - energy channels which represent our right and left hemispheres. But its practices are for the balanced persons who are merely 15%. They have both sides of their body strong. They exhaust later, never suffer from serious diseases and live longer.

The practices of any Yoga do not create balance, hence the imbalanced persons, including the Yogis, suffer at the end. They have one side of their body weak which suffers from diseases when the strong side is exhausted. Some persons are badly imbalanced. They suffer from incurable diseases. Only the weak side needs exercises. By general exercises and Yoga our strong side is activated and we think that we are completely healthy, while the weak side is neglected and dragged by it. We use the weak side as a clutch like a lame person. Ida and pingla when balanced dissolve in sushumana-the neutral channel which leads to meditation by it self.

2. "KNOW THYSELF"

Though this saying in the Bible is concerned with spirituality, it is better to begin with the body.

Know your imbalance in the left or right side of your body.

1. Test by breath

Watch your breath all the day. You will see that you breathe for a longer time by one nostril and less by the other. This is imbalance. If time is equal you are balanced. If you breathe by both the nostrils at a time, it is even worse than the imbalance because difficult to improve. When you want to do something, right breath starts but as you are not allowed to do it , it stops and the left begins. It creates tension and our breath by both nostrils is repeated. As a result we change our sides while sleeping or lying down.

If you breathe more by the right side your right side of body is strong and left side is weak. In the right side your breath goes more up and deep below and right lung fully expands, quite opposite is the case with the left side. Your right side maintains your body.

These facts are not taught in the respiratory system of medical science because it is curative, not preventive. This is the body language. This kowledge does matter in the case of health and diseases.

Test of the Child-

In Hindus, in the naming ceremony of a child, the father is told to keep his fingers on the nose of the child. This formality is done. It means, the father should watch the breathing style of the child for the whole day and should make effort for its balance.

Breathing style of a healthy and cheerful man is tested. He breathes for 90 minutes alternately by each nostril. This balance gives an efficiency in action and a good quality of rest. Breathing by each nostril may fluctuate up to 180 minutes. This balance is rarely found. Some people breathe by one nostril for one hour and by the other for 3 or 4 hours. Some are imbalanced to the extreme. I was breathing by right side for 23 hours a day and by left for one hour only. At the age of 65 I came to know it and struggled for 8 years for balance. I escaped from a serious disease of heart and lung. I have found such other persons also.

We breathe by the hemispheres. If those are healthy they work alternately. By hemispheres, I mean the energy body of the hemispheres. When one hemisphere goes up we breathe in, when it comes down we breathe out. Nose is only a passage. So we breathe by the brain. Some one has written papers "Brain Breathings".

2. Test by Hemispheres

Our brain is divided into two semicircles. 'Semi' is pronounced as 'hemi' in Greek language. Hemispheres control the opposite side of our body. Right controls the left side and the left controls the right side of the body.

1. If you feel pain in the right side of your head, your left side of body is weak and vice versa.
2. The strong hemisphere drags the body when we turn.

If you are told to move around and you move anticlockwise - it means your left hemisphere is dragging you towards the left. It is strong and your right side is strong. While walking you always turn by the left and going on the road your gaze will be towards the left, your head will be bent towards left side and vice versa. See the photograph of Mahatma Gandhi and Anna Hazare - their head is bent in the right side. Their left body is strong.

3. Test by the Vibrations of Hemispheres

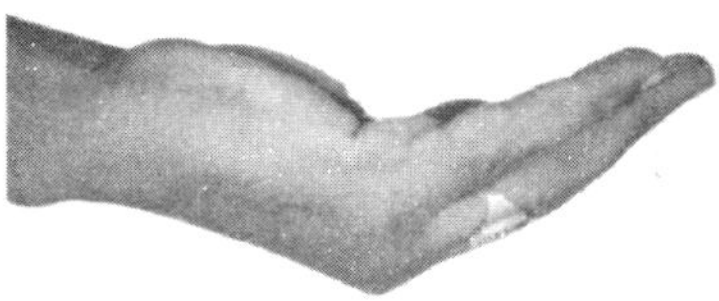

Spoon Shaped Hand

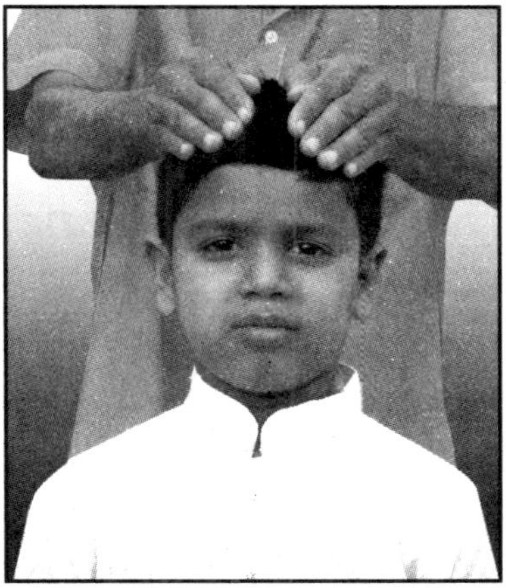

Make your palm spoon shaped and keep on the hemispheres alternately for a few minutes. You will see that on the one hemisphere the vibrations are prominent and regular like pulse - beating. The other hemisphere gives dull vibrations and you will feel the palm being pushed up due to the negative energy.

4. Test by the Legs

When you stand, the weight of your body is almost on one leg. If it is on the right leg, your right side of body is strong and vice versa. If your weight is more or less on both legs, it is just like breathing by both nostrils.

5. Test by Food

Our liver is on right side. It digests solid and heavy food. Ifyou can easily digest solid food, feeling no heaviness in the stomach, your right side is strong. Our spleen is on the left side. It digests liquids, fruits, vegetables and water. If you feel light by the liquids, your left side is strong. This difference is clearly seen in old age. Wheat is a heavy diet and rice is a light diet. In north India, wheat eating people, above 70% of them are having strong right side and in the south, rice eating people are generally having their left side strong.

The persons whose right side is strong, they feel less thirsty, consume less water. Their sweating is less and only restricted to the right side. They cannot observe fast. They are easily excited, angry and violent, always in hurry, restless and mechanical. The persons whose left side is strong, consume more water. They can take energy by water only. So they can observe long fasts. They are always calm and pacified, fond of fine arts and are spiritualists.

6. Test by Diseases

If you suffer from any disease on the right side and the left hemisphere connected by it, all your diseases will begin from the right side and vice versa. When disease increases, it goes on the other side. You will suffer from Sinusitis, Gas trouble, etc., on one side only.

7. Test by Pressing Yin Yang Chakras

The words 'Yin Yang' belong to Chinese language, but are accepted universally. 'Yin' means 'left side' - female energy of the moon. 'Yang' means 'right side' - male energy of the sun. These Chakras are below the collarbone, in the corner pits. Yin is in the left side and Yang on the right side. Press them with your thumb. You will see that one side is strong, its resistance is hard, one is weak, its resistance is poor, it feels pain.

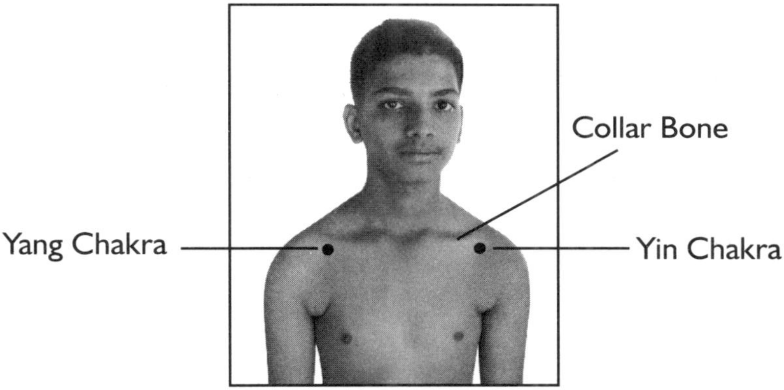

8. Test by Pressing the fleshy place between the thumb and index finger -

If you press this point you will see that strong side is more fleshy and solid and weak side is less solid and some times paining

9. Test by Aura Scanning

In the books of Reikei and Pranic Healing, the radiation of energy is shown around the body. The radiation in the strong side is more and on the weak side is less and even broken somewhere. This requires minute observation. This can be known by moving the fingers all over the body.

If the medical science develops some instrument for judging the weak side, there will be no need of these tests.

3. CLASSIFICATION OF THE LEARNERS

Yoga Master should classify the patients and the learners into three groups.

1. **L - Group :** The persons whose left side is weak, as the heart-patients They need exercises of left side of body and right hemisphere.

2. **R - Group :** The persons whose right side is weak, as the liver-patents. They need exercises of right side of body and left hemisphere.

3. **B - Group :** The persons whose both sides are balanced and also those whose both sides are weak. These persons need exercises of both sides. The persons who are suffering from Sinusitis on both sides of the nose and they have to breath by mouth. Their both sides are weak.

As we keep the record of our blood group, we should know our group for balancing.

In some cases both sides are partialy strong and weak. In this confusion accept B.Group friendship of the L Group persons with the R. Group persons will be intimate because both create a balance. B. Group presons are well -related with the B.Group.

4. INITIATION

In Yoga there is no initiation to the disciples. Without

initiation one cannot grow spiritually. There is no reference of initiation in Hatha Yoga or in the Yoga Darsan of Patanjali. Initiation is good even for health and general well being. It connects us with the Universal energy by which we are cut off. By initiation we receive continuously Universal energy as a blessing. Everybody should take initiation at the age of ten. It is as essential as the polio drops for the young children. For initiations, Reikei Masters are available nowadays. The traditional initiations such as entering in Sannyas are dead initiations. Reikei Master draws certain symbols on our body to remove the blocks and clears the way for Universal energy with which every cell of our body is illuminated and energised. You must pay fee to the Reikei Master after initiation. This energy exchange maintains the movement of the Universe, fortifies the relations, unburdens both the giver and receiver, thus creates a balance. Patanjali refers God as a Guru. But God will not come to give you initiation. In Hatha Yoga and Tantra, the importance of Guru is stressed but those kind of Gurus are not available nowadays. Moreover their behaviour with their disciples is dominating. The relation of a Guru and disciple should be friendly like that of Lord Krishna and Arjuna. This relation is based on love. Energy of Guru enters the eyes of the disciple and both are connected forever. This is a natural happening. We should wait for that moment. If there is no provision for initiation, you can go without it.

5. METHODS OF BALANCING

1. Breathe more by the nostril which flows less in proportion to the imbalance. Roll a strip of cloth and block the nose of the strong side. If you feel uneasy, remove the block for a short time and try again. Take it

off at the time of sleeping, eating and bathing. If you are not in a position to block your nose, breathe mentally by that side.

BLOCK THE LUNG

2. While sleeping keep the weak side of the body up. Breathing of the weak side will start, because the lower lung is blocked due to pressure of the upper side. It takes 10 minutes to change. It is the only way for the young children who cannot practice any other methods by themselves. Their mother should be more aware about this fact. After putting the child in the right position, see repeatedly whether the child is breathing properly or not ? If it is sinusitis patient, treat its disease.

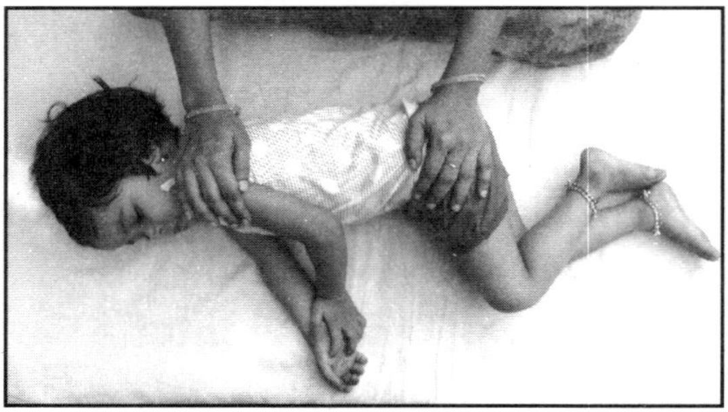

The child sleeping on the right side will breathe by the left nose and vice versa

3. Use a Yoga clutch. Put it under the armpit of the strong side and press gently. It activates the opposite hemisphere and starts the breathing of the weak side. Formerly saints used it in India. Here the lung dominates the hemisphere.

Yoga Clutch

Half Lotus Posture
& Shiv Ling Mudra
by the thumb for L-Group.
Energy entering the thumb
from above the Space.

4. **Half Lotus Posture:** Sit comfortably on the floor, chair or bed. Keep the leg of the weak side on the other thigh. You will see that this position pulls your opposite hemisphere and your required breathing will start.

5. **Shiv Ling Mudra:** Keep your thumb erect of the weak side of your body and fingers bent towards the palm for 45 minutes a day or 25 minutes twice a day or 15 minutes thrice a day. You can do it by sitting, standing or lying down. Right thumb takes energy from the Sun and left thumb takes energy from the Moon. You will feel in the due course of time, the negative energy going out of the thumb and fresh energy entering the body.

Veet Raag Mudra:

Half Lotus Posture & Veet Raag Mudra
of the palm for L-Group.
Energy entering the palm from
above the Space.
Here two methods are applied at the
same time. If the right nose is
blocked, the third method is also
applied.

You can keep the palm in a spoon shape of the weak side in the same manner. It also sucks energy from the Universe. Practise other mudras like wise by one hand only.

Balancing (Samanvay) Mudra -

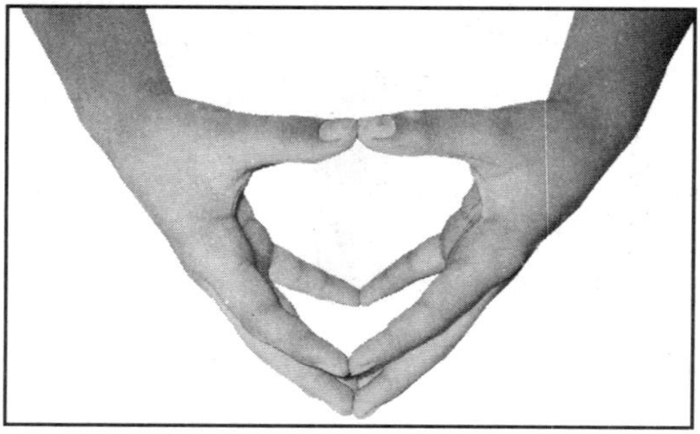

It is all in one and for all groups. Bring your hands facing each other and join the fingertips and thumbs together. Practice it for 45 minutes or 15 minutes thrice a day. It balances the weak parts of our body on both sides by supplying energy. Energy goes out from below the nails, by this mudra the energy returns and works in our body. That energy bears our intelligence and emotions. It knows us better than a doctor and a psychologist because it has worked within us. People think that the energy which goes out is negative and it should not be allowed to come in. This is true if a man is sick. If he is healthy the outgoing energy contains 50% positive energy which comes back and corrects our body and the negative energy goes out through other outlets. This is why the physical touch of the self or of a loving person gives us joy because it gives us energy. This mudra is popular in USA. If you are troubled by anybody's anger or his presence, this mudra will save you from his negative energy. It will not allow the outer negative energy to come in.

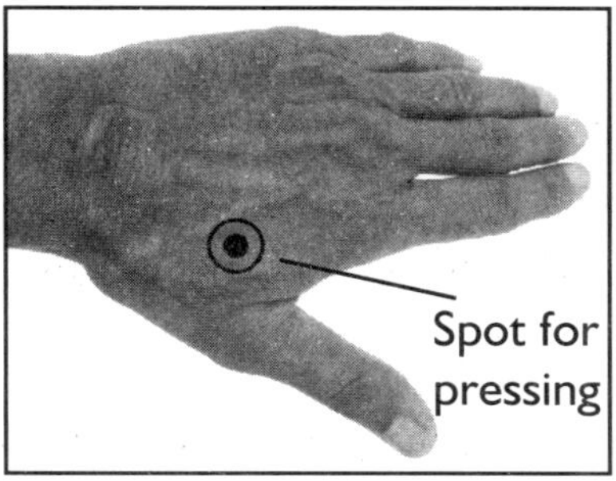

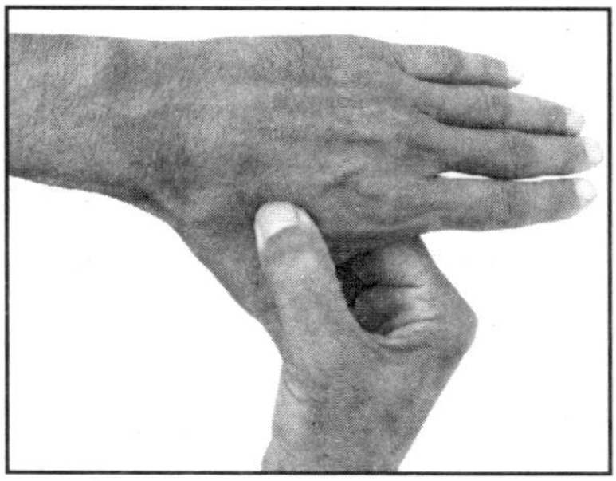

6. Pressing the fleshy part between the thumb and index finger - do it on the weak side of your body thrice a day from 2 to 4 minutes, 2 hours after meals. Press gently if weakness is normal and press hard if weakness is chronic. It energises the half side of the body. In Acupressure it is a point for curing constipation but it is also useful in this way. If you feel pain on this point put the hand in hot water mixed with salt for 15mintes and for one month. The pain of chest and lung comes in this point and is dissolved in the salt water.

7. Flick down the hand- stand and flick quickly your hand of the weak side for 5 mintes, twice a day. negative energy of the head chest goes out by the fingers, and fresh energy enter the part of the body.

8. Clapping- Mr. Krishna Chand Bajaj (New Delhi) popularised it as a general exercise, I have made it useful for balancing.

   Method- Sit on the chair, bare feet toching the earth. Apply oil to the palms. Keep the hand of strong side fixed and clapp with other. Do it for 5mintes or more. Clapp quickly and stop suddenly. Close your eyes and watch the peace within.

9. **Balancing by food:** If your left side is weak, avoid liquids, rice, curd, vegetables and more water till you are balanced. If your right side is weak avoid oily, heavy and solid food.

10. **Balancing by leg:** When you stand, put the weight of your body on the leg of the weak side. Jump by the leg of the weak side. If you play foot ball, kick by the leg of the weak side. Jumping by one leg was a game of children in India but they did not know by which leg to jump.

11. **Walking sideways:** Stand and walk towards your weak hemisphere to activate it and turn by the same and walk again. If your left side is weak, walk sideway towards the right, your right hemisphere will drag the left side and vice versa.

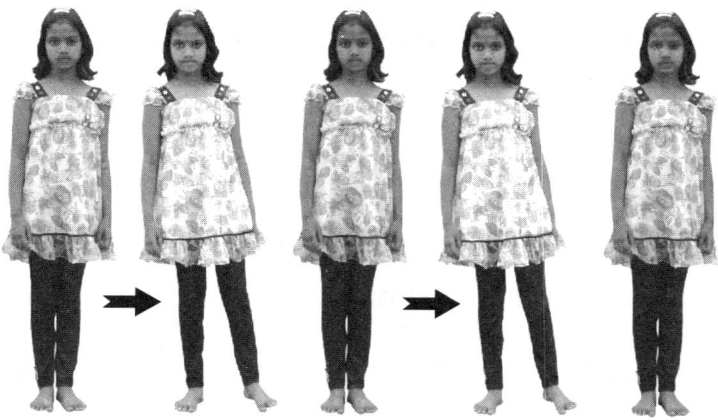

For R-Group. Walking towards the left hand & left hemisphere

12. For the B Group -1. Indian Games , Kabbadi, Aata Bata

and Kho, In these games the players have to move briskly towards right and left. This movement activates both the hemispheres of the brain. These games need a small ground and no material

II-Walking in a serpentine way- Chineses soldier walk towards right and left turning their face and body during parade. It is shown in Television it also activates both the hemispheres of the brain.

III- Walking in the shape of figure eight.

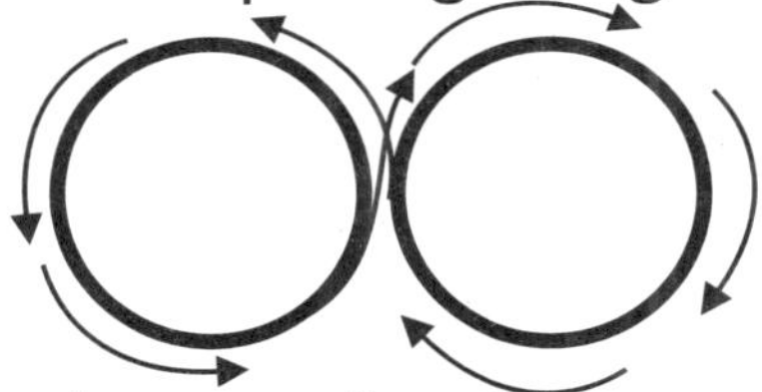

Stop Useless Long walks, Choose the walking style which you need.

13. Draw Reikei or Pranic Energy on the weak hemisphere at least for 3 minutes.

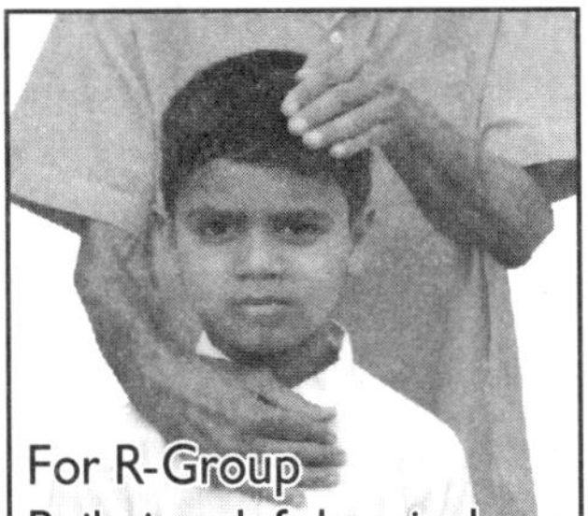

For R-Group
Reikei on left hemisphere

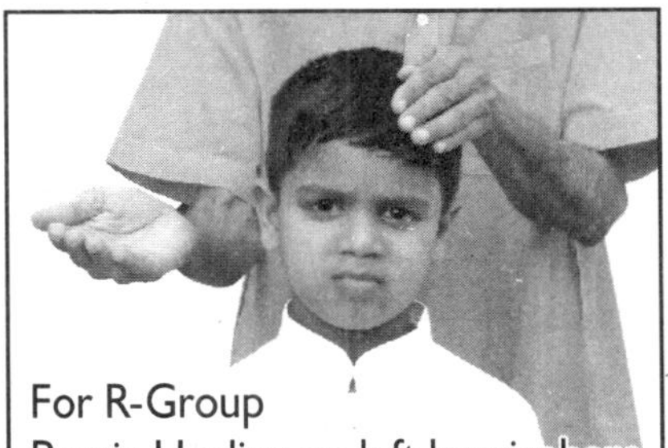

For R-Group
Pranic Healing on left hemisphere

14. **Micro Reikei:**

This is negative charge (Clockwise)

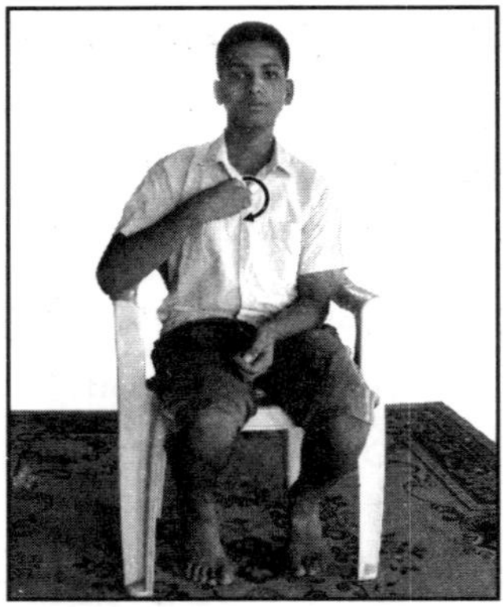

Curl your fingers and move on the Chakras or diseased part of the body anticlockwise for positive charge and clockwise for negative charge.

If your right side is weak give positive charge, if left side is weak give negative charge. In positive charge Chakras of the body receive energy from atmosphere and in the negative charge they throw out the waste energy from the body. For 7th, 6th and 5th chakras - give energy only for 3 minutes and on the lower chakras you can do for the more time. This activity can be done for you by some other person also.

15. **No Dimensions :** This is a Sufi Meditation. I propose only its half part for the imbalanced persons.

Method : If your right side is weak, it means your left hemisphere is weak. Stand and keep your left hand on the chest and right hand on the navel. Now take your right hand from navel and right foot forward and uttering "Shoo" bring back the hand and the foot. Then towards the right side, repeat the same. Now turn towards the left and do it again. Then again turn towards the left. Thus go on moving towards the left and taking your right hand and right foot forward and towards the right as much as you can. When tired, sit down on the chair or bed bare feet on the bare earth. This is the exercise of the right side and left hemisphere of your body. And if your left side is weak, do the exercise of left leg and hand and go on turning towards the right.

You should do all your physical activities by the weak side of body. And whenever turning is required, turn by the opposite side.

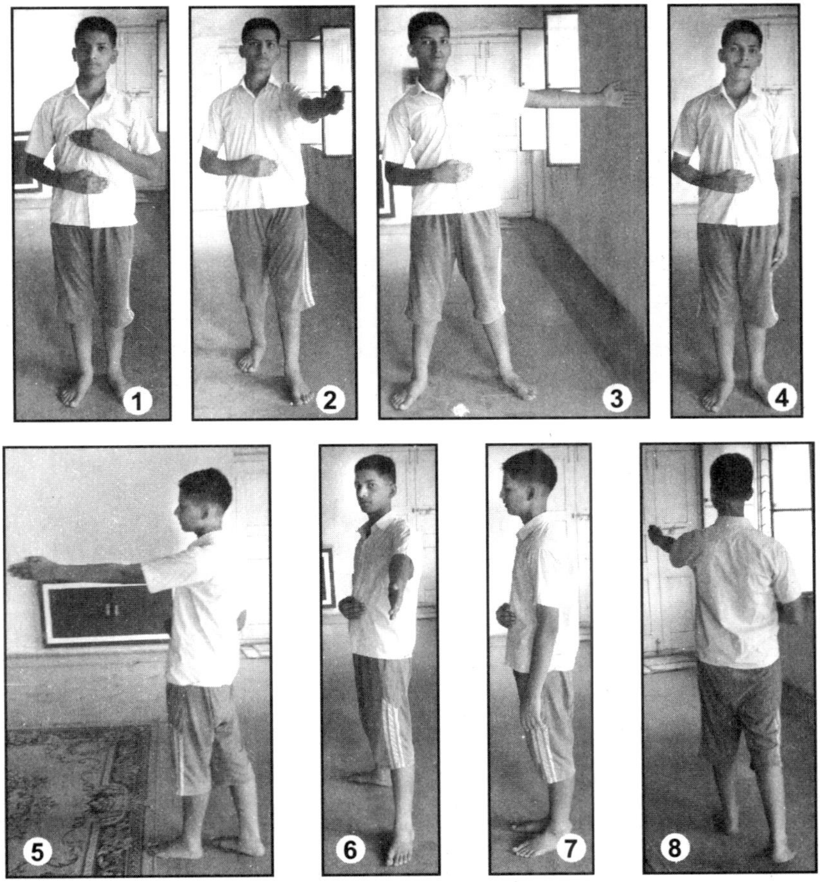

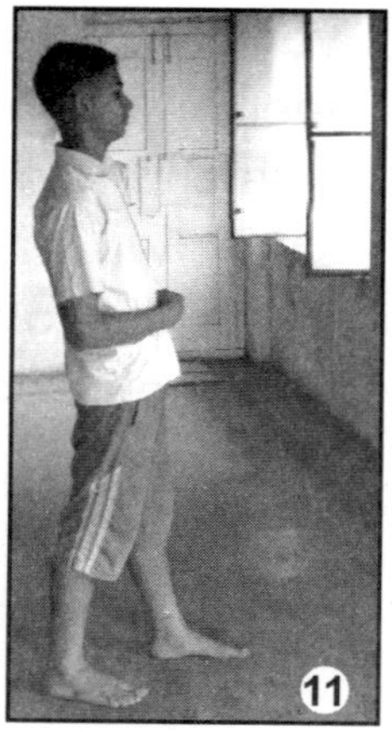

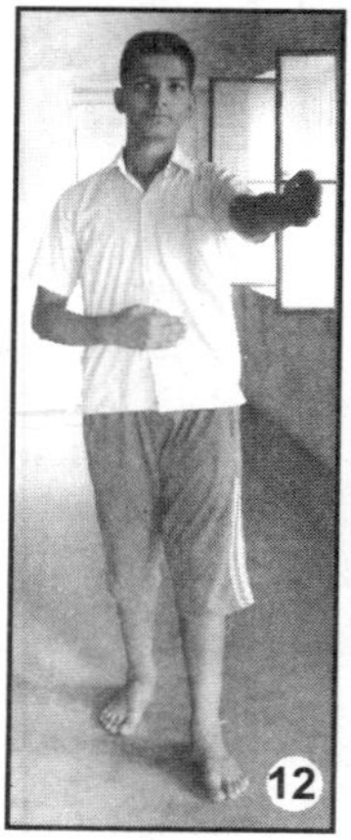

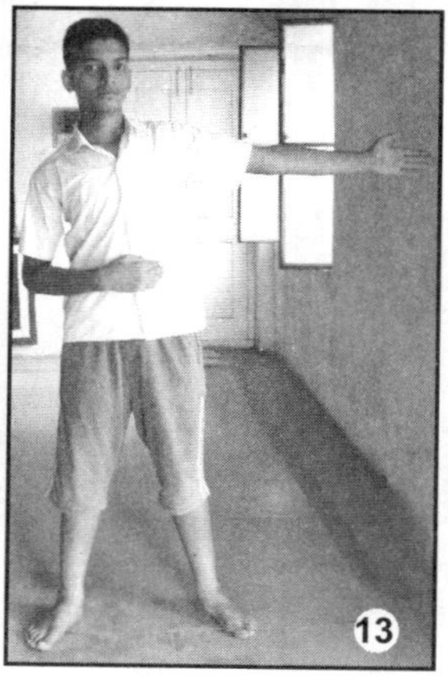

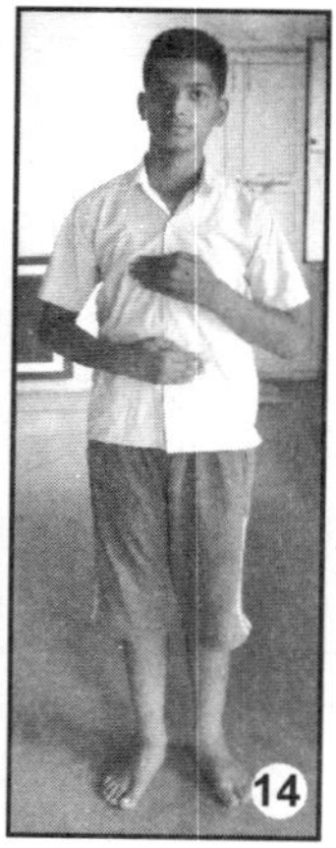

This is one round for L-Group & vice-versa for the R-Group Always keep the face in front.

16. **Parikrama- (Moving round)**

Put a stool or a chair in the centre of the room. Move around it clock wise or anti clock wise as you need. In hindu temples people move around temple clock wise. Anti is not allowed. That is only for the persons of L-group. In the temple of Lord Shiva there is drainage in the back side, people go clock wise upto the drainage and come back anti clock wise to that point again. They do it for 108 times. This is for B group.

17. **Whirling:** If your right side is weak, stretch your right palm facing the sky and the left palm below facing the earth and move anticlockwise (towards the left side). When tired, sit on the bed or chair bare feet on the bare earch. Energy rises from the root chakra and goes up to the head and flushes down the negative energy of the body through the feet in to the earth for purification. It is a positive charge .

Whirling : for R-Group

Spinning: If your left side is weak, do the vice versa. Stretch your left palm facing the sky and the right palm below facing the earth and move clockwise and when tired, sit down. It is negative Charge. Jalaludin Roomi was enlightened at the age of 18 by Spinning. He is the founder of it. He used to do it as a play from the very childhood.

It is popular in Sufis and Tibetans. Osho has included these methods in his meditations. George Gurdjieff used to give a show of it with a group of 100 persons. Some people think that whirling and spinning are one and the same thing. I have made a difference between 'whirling' and 'spinning' because these are quite opposite and activate our opposite hemispheres. I call it 'whirling' when we move anticlockwise and 'spinning' when we move clockwise. One should do it according to his need otherwise it is harmful to health and psychology. The hand which is up receives energy from the atmosphere and the hand which is low throws the energy after use. Moving around is a form of dance. All the Stars and Planets are in such a movement. Sufies practice spinning for hours together in the moonlit night till they faint and fall down. They copy Jalalu din roomi. Tibtens advise to move around for 21 times. Osho advises for 40 minutes. You should do it according to your capacity.

You can practice whirling or spinning by sitting. Sit comfortably on the ground or chair. Put your hands on the knees. Bring forward your head and move it towards the weak hemisphere thus making a half circle do it again. The hemisphere activates the connected part of the body and gives it energy. If you feel any trouble stop at once and begin again after being normal.

After all these activities, stop suddenly and close your eyes. Continue the period of stop so long you feel peaceful. The energy goes out by the activity and by the sudden stop it turns inward. This is called 'Pratyahar' in yoga. (Ref - 'Meditations' Part 3)

In the period of Stop you will realise that our both· hemispheres are connected at the sixth Chakra. The energy produced in one hemisphere goes to the other if surplus. So is the case with diseases.

When all the Chakras move you can see your aura moving. If it is powerful it will force your body to move as children do. Dolphin in the sea jumps and spins for three or four times. This is a sort of play, a joy.

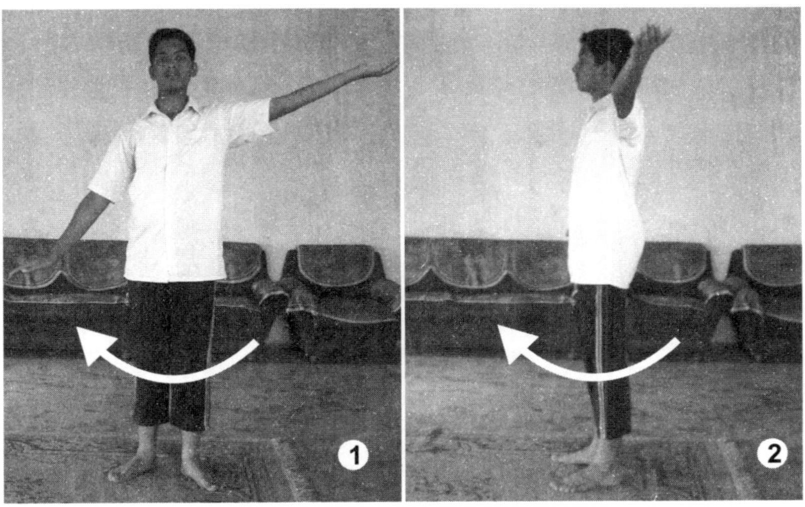

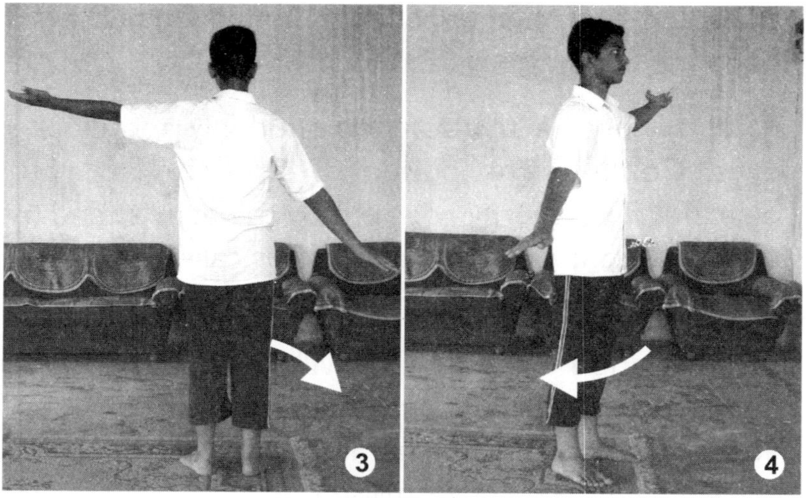

Spinning : for L-Group

18. **Rolling:** Lie down on a grassy ground and roll towards your weak hemisphere like children.

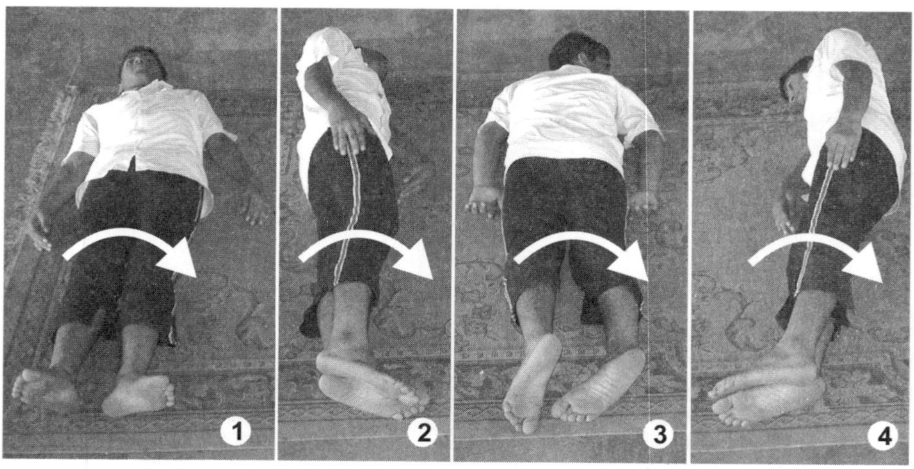

Rolling : for R-Group

19. **Slow motion movement -** Use your leg and hand of the weak side. Lie down, Move your foot , heel touching the earth, as slowly as possible up to the distance of one and half foot. Bring back leg slowly. Do it for three times.

II Bring your foot touching the earth towards the hip and take back slowly for three times.

III Take your hand, palm on the earth, from the hip moving towards the shoulder and stop at the angel of 90 degree. Bring back the hand slowly for three times.

IV Now stop and watch the affect within your body.

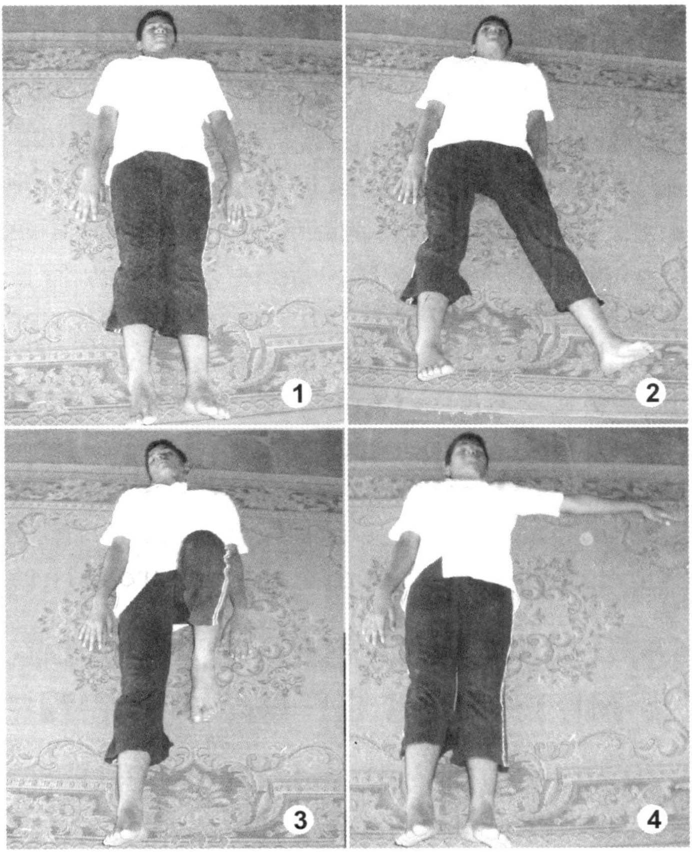

Apply all these methods, one or two will not do.

You will find the confusion in deciding right and left of the body and opposite hemispheres, after a few days you will clearly understand and will be settled. Have patience. Negative energy goes out by these exercises and fresh energy enters our body.

6. NEED OF TODAY

Nowadays it is a great problem to maintain health and mental peace throughout the life. The practices advised in this book give a new hope. These are experimented. These are meant for healthy persons. Sick persons should practice them slowly and comfortably. Don't over-strain your body. In the schools and colleges these exercises should be an essential part of physical training. These are better than games. These exercises should be introduced in the Military Parade to keep the soldiers fully healthy. General Ayub Khan, President of Pakistan could not receive the salute of Army in a function during 1965 as his right hand was paralised. His right side of body must be weak. These practices are preventive. If people adopt these exercises, in future the world will be free from serious diseases. The approaches which are unbalanced are partial. Achieving balance is a wholistic approach in the real sense. Start balancing in time and be safe forever. Preventive methods are more important than the research of medicines.

7. IMBALANCE OF BREATH - IN & OUT & METHODS OF BALANCING

Our life proceeds by expanding and shrinking. When we breathe in our nerves expand, when we breathe out our nerves shrink. There should be a balance between both expanding and shrinking. But here too, we are imbalanced. In traditional Yoga breathing exercises called Pranayama are not based on balance.

Test of imbalance: Slowly take your breath in, hold, note the time in seconds and your mental condition. Now be normal and again breathe out completely, hold and watch the psychology. About 70% people in our country take more breath in and hold within for a longer time feeling happy and breathe out less and find difficult and suffocating by holding out. This is due to accumulative tendency. By such breathing, the air which remains in lungs, goes on being congested below and below and causes diseases at the end.

They expand themselves more and shrink less. This structure of body at the time of death assumes such condition that they take the breath in but cannot throw out. So it is said about them "he breathed his last".

Method : For such 70% people Kapal Bhati Pranayam is essential, not for everybody. Osho's dynamic meditation is the best and complete form of Kapal Bhati (Dragon Breath) attended by meditation as a byproduct. Here we have to breathe out deeply, repeatedly and hurriedly. Begin by breathing out. Indian classical Music and chanting the mantras are the forms of Kapal Bhati. Indian game Kabbadi is also a form of it. In it the player has to pronounce one word continuously as long as he can.

About 15% people naturally breathe out more and take in less. They shrink more and expand less. They are broad-minded, philanthropists or spendthrifts or helpful to others.

Method : They need to take breath in deeply and should not care about throwing out. They should begin by breathing in. About such people it is said "he expired". At the time of their death, their breathing organs shrink and cannot breath in. Due to these tendencies both types of persons suffer from certain diseases during their life.

If they are heart patients they should breathe by left and if they are liver patients they should breathe by the right nose. This is the basic and permanent treatment. The other treatments are necessary but temporary as our Prime minister Dr. Mohan Singh has undergone by-pass surgery of the heart for the second time last year.

Doctor advises the heart patients to take bed rest. If the patient is not breathing by the left nose his rest will be a restlessness. Merely physical rest will no do. Mental rest is attended by the left breath.

About 15% people are balanced. They take in and out in same proportion. For them Bhastrika Pranayam is suitable. They should take breath in and out equally, deeply and quickly.

Limit of all these practices is 10 minutes a day. After such breathing, laugh at once for the same time. It may be artificial, otherwise the energy arisen from the abdomen will hit the heart and make it weak. By laughter energy goes out from the throat and heart is saved.

A sinusitis patient who cannot breathe by one side of the nose, should practice other exercises of the same side. If both sides of his nose are blocked and the patient is a mouth breather, he should practice both-side exercises like the balanced persons.

First type of people who need Kapal Bhati should also practice outward Bharmari (Humming with breathing out). Second type of people should practice inward humming. Third type of people should practice both. Humming should be practiced for about 30 minutes a day, twice or thrice. It opens seventh Chakra. It is the essence of om.

For the balanced persons Anulom Vilom or vice versa (Cross breathing exercise) is suggested.

Method : If your left side is weak, take in breath by the left nose and breathe out by the right, then breathe in by the right and breathe out by the left. If your right side is weak, begin by the right side and release by the left. Then take by the left and release by the right. Repeat it for 10 minutes.

Everyone, even the imbalanced persons can do it for 3 minutes after meals and after 2 hours they can practice it for 10 minutes. It helps in balancing and if you are balanced, it maintains balance. It activates our both hemispheres alternately and our digestive system of solid and liquid begins to work. Don't do it empty stomach. It will create heat in the brain and stomach.

8. BALANCING DIET

Cooking should be balanced. A few women know proper cooking otherwise the food is either over cooked or under cooked. In both cases it is harmful to health. According to medical science there should be six elements in our balanced diet. Proteins, fats, Carbohydrates, Vitamins, Mineral salts, Enzymes etc., According to Ayurveda the balance of six *Rasas* as Sweet, Saltish, Bitter, Sour, Pungent and

Astringent should be properly balanced. Here balance means required proportion, not equal. We can take sweet and salt daily and the other *rasas* should be taken once or twice a week. Further there should be balance in the three humours (*Kaph, Vat, Pitt*) - phlegm, air and bile (black & yellow). Our bodily weight should be balanced as required.

Balancing Mudra balances all the elements, rasas and humours in our body. The surplus one is thrown out and the required one is preserved and produced. You can practice it after meals or later in the sitting position or lying down.

Balance in family, society and nations should be properly observed according to the needs of everybody. Bank balance maintains the economical balance of families, institutions and nations. Everybody should have a bank balance. In Banking balance means the remaining amount.

9. BALANCING YOGA OF LORD KRISHNA

In Gita chapter 2, verse 48 Lord Krishna says to Arjuna "Balancing is Yoga", "*Samatvam Yoga Uchyate*". Similarly in Veda it is said - maintain balance in human and divine life. But this definition of Lord Krishna was overlooked and forgotten because the teaching of Lord Krishna was psychological in maintaining the peaceful attitude in the sorrows and joys. Joys and sorrows are only skin-deep. They come and go by themselves like day and night. Instead of balancing, we stick to joys forcibly and want to get rid of sorrows as soon as possible. There is nothing physical. People want something physically to do. I have done that work. I have developed physical exercises attached with that psychology.

10. MODERATION

"Be moderate in eating, sleeping walking and other worldly affairs. Do all the activities within limits. Don't overstrain your body or mind" (Gita - 6-17). Nowadays we respect the persons who go in the extreme. Energy moves towards the opposite pole. If you have gone towards one extreme, you will have to go to the other extreme. Thus you will always fluctuate between the two extremes. Extremity creates imbalance, tension and makes the life a feverish activity full of diseases and sorrows. Once I saw a beggar sitting on the road in the noon time in summer season. His legs were swollen like the legs of an elephant. I wondered how he is living in such a wretched condition. He is tolerating this trouble because he must have been lived an extremely luxurious life in the past. It is just like avoiding the dinner if you have overeaten in the lunch time. It is your need. We cannot escape from the troubles but we can be moderate in enjoyments. Some people who have extremely enjoyed, search troubles for themselves, such as going deep in the seas, jumping from the high mountains. Lord Buddha, being a prince adapted a beggarly life. Life is like a music and poetry. It is not a mathematical calculation. If you accept the middle path, you can save yourself from the extremity and by transcending duality you can reach the third stage of Bliss.

Lord Buddha learnt by his experience that the middle path is the only way to live happily and grow spiritually. The strings of guitar, if compressed more than required are broken. If let loose more than required, they cannot produce music. If they are tightened in the middle way, the music is produced. So is the case with life.

11. UPASANA (POSTURES - ASAN)

Yoga is completely identified with the postures and breathing exercises. Lotus posture is the symbol of Yoga. An exponent of postures is considered as a Yoga Master. These postures are practiced by memory in a planned order. Memory can never lead us to awareness or meditation and energy blocks remain in the body as they are. The best and spiritual way for the postures is in Osho's 'Upasana Meditation'.

Physical Upasana : 'Upasana' means 'to sit near'. People think that they should sit near the God. But here you sit near yourself, be in your own company. Go in a closed room. Sit or lie down as you like. Do nothing. After sometime or some days you will feel doing something. When we are free and peaceful, the energy blocks (suppressed energy of emotions) arise and force us to do something. So do something according to your inner call. For example you may like to stand and bend your body sideways or front and back, you may like to jump, you may like to move your hands or legs - do it in anyway you like. Thus postures will happen by themselves and the suppressed energy will get an outlet. If you want to sleep, sleep. Practice this meditation for one hour. The blocks will melt and will be dissolved. It is your private life. You should do whatever you want. But in the public life you have to maintain the discipline. This is physical Upasana.

Physical Upasana : Substitute for Postures. Don't copy this.
Find out within your own positions.

Oral Upasana : According to culture and customs we are prohibited to speak many things. That suppression becomes a powerful energy block especially in the throat. Sometimes we cannot speak even the truth, that block creates diseases. In oral Upasana speak out whatever you like. Don't think wether it is good or bad. It will unburden your mind and dissolve the block. Sigmund Freud cured psychological diseases by telling his patients to speak freely for an hour or two. By Yoga postures our energy blocks do not come in action and there is no possibility that they will ever dissolve.

APPENDIX

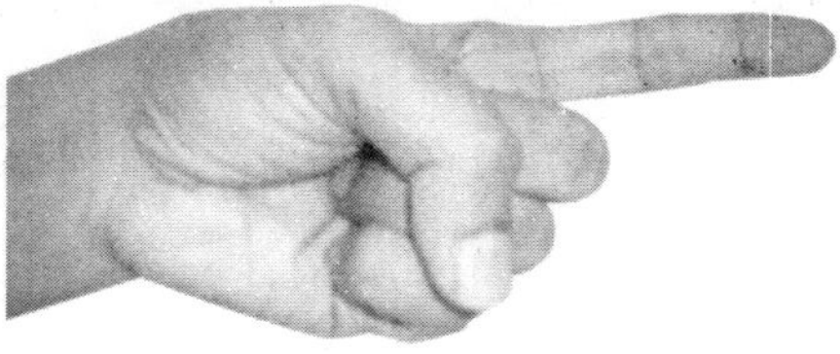

1. INDEX FINGER

The index finger emits powerful but destructive energy. Don't use it for cleaning the teeth or nose. Don't put it in the ears. Don't allow the young child to catch hold of it while walking. In breathing exercises if you touch the nose by it, it creates itching. In breathing exercise use your thumb to close one side of the nose and keep the index finger bent at the end of the thumb and use the middle finger for this purpose. Generally we use it for a very short time, so its harm is not observed but it should be avoided in any case. It is used to ward-off the evil spirits. It is the base of *Sudarshan Chakra* of Lord Krishna.

2. IMBALANCE - PAST AND FUTURE

Imbalance follows even in the next birth and we get birth by the same type of imbalanced parents. So nothing is hereditary. This is a complex phenomenon. Some children are born sick, some suffer from acidity at the age of 7 days. Some have a hole in the heart or a damaged valve. These are the signs of their past life. Main disease is imbalance. Other diseases are its by-products. If imbalance is overlooked, medicines fail in the end and disease occurs again. We should struggle for balance even in old age, in any situation.

If the imbalance has happened in this life, your parts of body on both sides are equally developed. If the imbalance has followed you from the past life, your parts of body of the weak side are under-developed, just as eye, chest, arm and nose-hole etc. Some persons are having half face short, which seems perverted.

If you are balanced at present, it does not mean that you will remain balanced forever. Imbalance can occur at any time due to tension. So check your balance every month and maintain it.

3. LOTUS POSTURE (PADMASAN)

It is a posture in Hath Yoga for balance because both crossed legs pull our hemispheres. It is very troublesome and unnecessary for the imbalanced persons and not useful even for the balanced persons because the flow of energy going down is stopped. Same is the case with Vajrasan. Our energy should flow from heels to head and vice versa. For this purpose you can sit on the chair or bed or lie down in Sarala Asan - easy posture like a child, legs stretched and hands upon the knees.

4. BREATH - DAY

We have to struggle for balancing in proportion to our imbalance. The strong side does not allow to disturb its breathing. So sometimes we have to remove the block in the nose otherwise we feel suffocated. At such times remove the block and try again. In summer season the air is thin and contains less oxygen. It becomes difficult to balance. At that time we should practice *Anulom* or *Vilom* as we need. Close the nose of the strong side with your thumb and breath from the weak side, then breathe out by the strong side. Go on repeating it. *Anulom Vilom* is also called *Chandrabhedi* and

Suryabhedi. And when it is practiced with holding the breath after inhalation and after exhalation, then it is called *Nadi Shodhan*. *Nadi Shodhan* should be done for 10 times only. It removes blocks. Holding breath forcibly is harmful. Do it as easily as you can. The period of holding increases by itself with normal practice.

When you are successful in balancing breath, you will feel that you are born again. Celebrate your 'Breath - Day' instead of your birthday.

It is said that the last meditation of Lord Buddha was 'Vipassana' (watching the breath and allied objects). Buddha was enlightened by desirelessness. Desire is the major energy-block. Energy-blocks disturb our breath. When energy-blocks are removed, man is balanced and enlightened at once. We cannot copy Lord Buddha because our mind is full of desires. Our 'Vipassana' will be impotent though we may feel some physical benefit and mental peace. Balancing gives both physical as well as spiritual benefits.

5. SUN & MOON BREATH

Once a physiotherapist asked me "Hatha Yoga declares that breathing with right nose produces heat in the body and breathing by left nose produces coolness. How is it possible? Because both the nostrils meet at the end, temperature of air is same for both nostrils." I answered - "We cannot feel nor control the workings of hemispheres, liver and spleen but we can feel and control the breathing of our right and left nose. Right nose is connected with the left hemisphere. Left hemisphere activates all the right side of our body. So the lever which represents Sun, produces heat. Actually the heat is produced by the lever but it is known by the right breath. Similarly when we breathe by the left nose our right hemisphere activates our left side of body. In the left side there is spleen, which represents moon, which gives coolness. So it is said that left nose produces coolness. In the cold weather if you are shivering or you have to awake in the night or you want some extra energy for any hard activity, start breathing by the right nose. If you are troubled by the heat and fever or lack of sleep, breathe by the left nose. You will feel relief within an hour. George Gurdjieff lived amongst the gypsies in his childhood. He noted when they walked in the hot dessert in the summer season they breathed in a different way and in the cold winter their breathing style was changed, became quite opposite. Right and left breath are propellers of hemispheres and vice versa.

6. LAUGHTER AS YOGA

1. When we laugh, it may be artificial we breathe out more. This is a form of 'dragon breath' (*Kapal Bhati*).

2. When we laugh, all our parts of stomach shrink inside and energy moves upward. This is natural '*Uddyan Bandh*' (Flying-Lock).

3. When we laugh our energy goes out through the throat and heart becomes safe. Otherwise after *Kapal Bhati* if we keep silent, that energy will hit the heart and make it weak.

4. **Psychological benefit :** By laughing, our suppressed energy of enjoyments is released and makes our energy-

blocks nil. We get relief from the tension. While laughing we are thoughtless. This stage is called awareness or a meditation. If your laughter is artificial, it becomes real after three or four days because our suppressed energy begins to come out. After laughing stop suddenly and be silent. Close your eyes and maintain this condition of meditation as long as you can. Dr. Chopra, Director of Heart Care Foundation in Delhi says, one who laughs for 10 minutes a day cannot suffer from heart attack.

CRYING : The layers of energy blocks of joy and sorrow are heaped in our body one upon the other. When the layer of laughter is exhausted, the layer of crying comes over, then you will feel sad and you will like to cry. Then begin to cry. Lie down on your knees, head and hands touching the earth and try crying. After some days crying will be real and you will feel fresh after crying. Time of laughter is early in the morning. If you laugh in the morning, you will see that a wave of joy is coming in your heart all the day. Time of crying is evening. Just shut the room and there should be a little darkness. The laughing and crying are the psychological treatments. Their course is at least of two months. We are relieved of so many diseases by it, especially of the eyes. And there is a great peace and calm in our heart. Crying is a 'scream therapy'.

Laughter reminds happy incidents and crying reminds sorrowful events of life. We can take out the suppressed joys and sorrows from within and can balance them. Laughter and crying maintain the freshness our body.

7. HESITATION FOR THE NEW

In science, the truth is always in the present. In literature and religion, truth is always in the past, present is neglected and ridiculed. In this reference, it is interesting to read the satire 'Battle of Books' by Jonathan Swift. In a library the battle begins. The workers of the library are divided into two groups, one supports the ancient and the other supports the new books. They begin to throw out the books they dislike. Within it there is an episode of 'Bee and Spider'. Bee represents the past, which seems sweet as honey and the spider represents present time, which seems ugly and poisonous.

Sanskrit poet Kalidas writes in his play 'Malavika Agnimitram' - "All the past is not true just because it is old. New poetry is not condemnable just because it is new. The wise decide themselves and accept the truth, it may be in the present or past while the ignorant believe in others."

I have changed the structure of Yoga in this book. The wise will understand and accept it. But still they will find it difficult to practice because their flow of energy is not accustomed to it. They are advised to leave their old practices for few days and take rest. The old flow will subside. When the inner call inspires you to do something, start these practices. Your energy pattern will change and you can adapt easily the new practices. It will transform your life.

INDEX

PART II

Psychological Balance

1. DAILY PRAYER

In the prayers people speak some words in the praise of God and ask for his blessings. In the love we are connected with somebody. Prayer is the next step beyond the love. Prayer means to be connected with a higher energy and extending our love to all creatures.

Our fourth Chakra is the seat of human love and seventh Chakra which unites us with the Universe is the seat of divine love, the love of God. Master Choa Kok Suie proposes 'Twin-Heart Meditation'. Join your fingertips of right hand and move around the chest. Remember the love given by your parents and other persons. Then pronounce 'Om' two times. See the gap between the two 'Om's. After saying one 'Om' be silent and see that the energy goes up to the seventh. That is the response of God. Then move your fingers on the seventh Chakra. Thus your energy of fourth and seventh Chakras will unite and will make a way for spirituality.

On the earth there is always a time for prayer somewhere. People of different regions are engaged in the prayers. In imagination join their group. It will connect you with the higher energy.

WHITE LIGHT IMAGINATION :

"I know the Purush of white colour, beyond darkness. One who knows it transcends the death. That is the only way to salvation"

- Rigveda & Yajurveda
Gita 8/9

Invoke God, otherwise dangerous. Angels come when invited but evil spirits come uninvited. When we begin any meditation the passage of energy from our seventh Chakra becomes clear up to the lowest Chakra. If we do not invoke God evil spirits will enter our body.

Method : Imagine the divine energy of white colour above your head. It is entering your seventh Chakra, filling your all the body and flushing down the negative energy into the earth for purification. After a few months you will feel light and energetic. This is a best form of prayer. It should be done early in the morning when we get up. Nowadays a torch of white light is available. We can throw its light on all the Chakras and parts of body, it also gives energy. As the mother loves and kisses her child, so the mother earth also requires our touch. This is called healing or blessing the earth. For this purpose, our body should be filled by enormous energy by the meditations. So long as we are not in that condition, we should maintain this habit. Nowadays, earth is suffering from 1^0 temperature (Global Warming). When it will go up to 4^0 or 5^0 human life will be impossible.

Healing the Earth : In the end of this meditation, put your hands and forehead upon the earth, fingers of the feet touching the earth. Earth sucks up our negative energy and gives us fresh energy.

DARK ENERGY MEDITATION :

It should be done at the sleeping time at night. Dark (black) energy is earthly energy which has created our body and the Universe.

Method : Imagine the darkness like the clouds is arising from the root Chakra of your heels and coming upward towards the head. All your body and room is filled with darkness and go to sleep. It will keep you fresh and healthy. It gives a sound sleep.

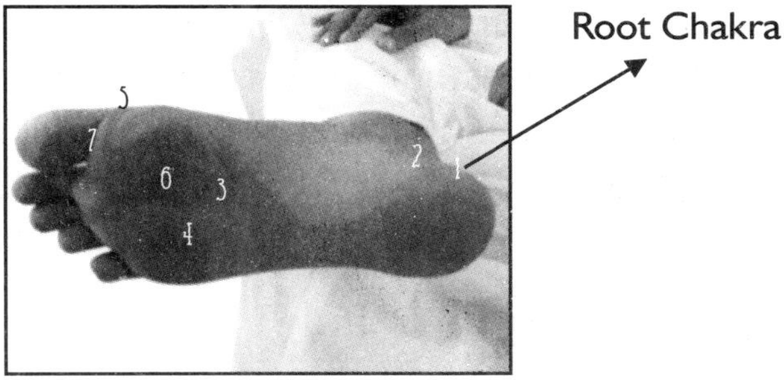

Chakras in the Foot sole

2. CONCEPT OF YOGA

Man has crossed animal lives and further he will join the life of angels and then he will be enlightened. Thus there are so many levels of energy. In *Sanskrit* '*yuj*' means to unite and people say Yoga means union with God. At present Yoga means uniting with an upper energy and God is far away. We feel happy when our energy joins some distant object of love. William Wordsworth says "My hear leaps up when I behold a rainbow in the sky". He is joined with nature. This joining with higher energy is the beginning of Yoga. Wordsworth entered ecstacy in the lap of nature. He says "our corporal frame is almost suspended and we become a living soul." His experiences are those of a Yogi. Similar is the case of a Hindi poet Sri Sumitranandan Pant. He says in his poem 'Silent Invitation' that the rising wave of the sea and the peeping moon through his window call him for company. In mathematics Yoga means 'total'. In medical science Yoga means a 'compound' and in astrology Yoga means 'a group of stars'.

Yoga is related with religion, (Yoga is the only religion) so it must have some spiritual quality. If the Yoga exercises fail to give us any spiritual experience, that is not Yoga at all. Nowadays definition of Yoga is limited to certain postures and breathing exercises only. The person who has some spiritual achievements should be included in the definition of a Yogi just like Lord Buddha, Lord Mahavira, Guru Nanakdev, Gorakhnath etc.,

Controlling the mind-

Mind is a by -product of our circumstances and limitations. When we are not allowed to do any thing our energy stops and is stored in the form of heat, pain or numbness. Thus there are so many energy blocks in our body, even of the past lives. This group of suppressed emotions and desires is called sub-conscious mind, which is the cause of diseases and cycles of rebirth. It is dust on the mirror of soul and can be polished by reike and other balanced exercises and meditations. At present we act according to the dominant block which is called conscious mind. Man is enlightened when all these blocks are exhausted or dissolved. So controlling means post poning again the thoughts which are already controlled. Mystics say don't control but polish the mirror of soul and get freedom forever. Words dissolving or polishing are used in literature out of ignorance. Nothing is perishable according to the law of conservation of energy in Physic. Negative energy becomes useful and co-operates with the positive, as the medicines are prepared by refining poison.

3. HISTORY OF YOGA

In the beginning of the fourth chapter of Gita, Lord Krishna says to Arjuna that Yoga is as ancient as humanity itself. In the due course of time it was forgotten. The same ancient Yoga of balancing, Lord Krishna told to Arjuna, and again it was forgotten. Balance of breath has its base in svar-yoga. Svar means heaven or Bliss. The word svarg is derived from it. Breath can lead us to heaven. So its name is svar-yoga. The Yoga and Tantras which are prevalent nowadays, their originator is Lord Shiva, who was king of Bhutan. He told all these Yogas to his wife and disciple Parvati. Svar-yoga is also told by Lord Shiva.

4. YOGA ANATOMY

Chakras (Introduction)

"Vehicle of human body has seven wheels pulled by seven horses"

- Veda.

In Sanskrit Chakra means a wheel. These are energy centres where energy moves like a wheel. The chakras are in the back bone. If activated those get energy from the universe. There are mainly seven chakras. Some people think that chakras are fictitious. Hirsohi Motoyama, doctor of Acu - punture in Japan has made a machine which shows the working of chakras.

Chakras move anti clokwise and up and down when they receive energy and circulate it to the upper and lower chakras. When they project negative energy of the body they move clockwise in their fixed places. The first is positive and the second is negative charge.

Channels

According to Tantra books there are 72 thousand energy channels in body connected with chakras and organs. These channels receive energy from chakras and supply to the body parts.These are not blood vessels but ethereal and can be photographed by high frequency camera. Amongst these the following three channels are important.

1. Pingla 2. Ida 3. Sushumana.

All these begin from root chakra. Pingla and ida go up to 6th chakra touching each chakra in a serpentine way. Pingla is of red color, ida of yellow and sushumana of white.(Reikei)

1.Pingla employs us in physical activity, material pleasures,logic and struggle. Its organ is liver. It is a solar energy. It is connected with left hemisphere of the brain, when it works our right side is active. This can be known by the breathing of right side of nose and can be thus controlled. It has a mechanical property, because it activates our motor organs. Its working is positive charge.

2.Ida gives us rest, creative pleasures like music or poetry and fine arts. Its knowledge is intuitive. It is connected with the left side of the body and with the right hemisphere of the brain, can be known and controlled by left side breathing of nose. It activates and keeps the left side of the body healthy. It is lunar. Its organ is spleen. It controls the sense organs of the body. Its working is negative charge.

3.Sushumana - when both ida and pingla are balanced the third channel sushumana becomes active. It contains and controls both and gives awareness. First two channels end in 6th chakra. These keep us in worldly activity. Sushumana gives us awareness and leads to vastness and oneness. After 6th chakra ida stops and pingla as a vehicle, goes with sushumana. It leads us in the middle and front head, universal and personal awareness. When we are traveling in the train we are active and restful both. Such is the function of sushumana. As there is an earth - point in the plug, so sushumana is space - point in the bio - electricity. It is neutral.

It contains the qualities of joy and sorrow. Here seriousness becomes serenity. Working of sushumana can be known by the equal and simultaneous breathing by both nostrils. Breath becomes so soft and thin that it seems almost nil. Pingla digests solid food, ida liquid, and sushumana needs no food. So there is no desire for eating and drinking, or anything else. There are some people who do not take anything for days and months together.

Aura

"It is not the eyes or nose or lips we beauty call,
But the total and joint impression of all".

- Alexander Pope

"She walks in beauty"

- Lord Byron.

There is something around our body. Matter has an etheric charge (ionized gas, plasma) around it. In living beings it is called aura in Latin, bio-plasma in Russian and Tejas in Sanskrit language. This is energy field scattered by our chakras. This is also called vital force or astral body. Animals and trees also have their aura. It is about one inch in side our body (as chakras are) and about two inches out side. It is called inner aura. In a healthy man its rays are spread up to three feet. Those are called health rays or outer aura. It is our shadow even in the darkness. Commonly it is called soul which has non-physical presence. Some people have written books on "Body Electronics".and "Human Astomphere" about the aura. There are 4 layers of aura around our body. To some people the group of energy channels gives a feeling of aura within our body. The developed auras are like the spread out feathers of a dancing peacock.

1. **The vital aura**- It is called Pranamaya Kosh in sanskrit. It is formed by the energy rays of first and second chakra. Vital aura is yellow in colour and develops around the Trees, animals and illiterates.
2. **Mental aura** - called Manomaya Kosh in Sanskrit. It is formed by 3rd chakra and red in colour. It enables us to receive the education given by the society and to think about past and future. One can notice the difference between the educated and illiterate persons, both have different personality and act differently.
3. **Emotional aura** (Vignanmaya Kosh) - (Here vignan does not mean science). It is formed by 4th chakra. As love is the seat of 4th chakra, this aura is developed by love added by meditations which is green in colour. This can extend to aura of the earth, as our speed increases in the train during traveling.Here astral traveling is possible. Then one can say soham - "I am That". The persons who glide in the air with the help of a parachute or a glider within the core of their

heart they have the desire for astral traveling. Some of them die. Meditations of fourth chakra are required for their survival. Eienstein imagined the journey at the speed of light. It will be possible by astral traveling.

4. **Cosmic aura** (Ananda maya kosh) - when one realizes awareness endlessness, bliss and delight he identifies himself with the universal aura. It is formed by the sixth chakra, and is in dark blue colour. Body becomes super conductor of universal energy. Universal aura is called Hiranaya Garbh in Sanskrit.

Halo - In sanskrit it is called Ojas. When the rays of energy extend up to 6 inches on the 7th chakra, the grandeur is called halo. Crowns are poor replica of the halo. These auras can be photographed by Kirlian photography. In every activity of life be conscious of your aura throughout the day. You will feel delighted and dignified in your actions.

Aura goes out of the body in the dream, and gets connected with the dominent chakra and comes back through it. Be aware when you wake up out of a horror dream, you will see something entering your body and that is returning of aura. Scanning and sweaping of aura is essential in pranic healing but optional in Reikei because Reikei is an intelligent energy and flows to other parts of body when overdosed. Pranic energy is not loving and intelligent, works like a machine and makes a pranic conjestion. There are chakras, channels and auras in every cell of our body. This is a grand design.

5. CHAKRA MEDITATIONS

Common to all Chakras are the concentration on the location of Chakra, drawing Reikei on it and chanting its sound (*Beeja Mantra*).

1. ROOT CHAKRA : It is in perineum. Its sound is 'Lam'. Chant it for at least 40 minutes a day. Honest earning and fearlessness make it strong. Perineal Lock (*Moola Bandha*) - Shrink and let loose its nerves for ten times. It melts the negative energy and releases it.

2. Hara (Swadhishtan) : It is located at the end of the backbone. It is nourished by the moderate enjoyments and making relationships and if one has no relationship and lack of enjoyment this Chakra will become weak. Its sound for chanting is 'Vam'.

3. Navel (Manipur) : It is located in the backside of the navel in the backbone. Its sound is 'Ram'. Flying lock (*Uddiana Bandha*), sense of domination and self assertion when required, social education, walking and running are its meditations.

4. Heart Chakra (Anahad) : It is located in the backbone behind the center of the chest. Its sound is 'Yam' and 'Soham'. Enjoying fine arts, greenery and love are helpful in its flowering.

5. Throat Chakra (Vishuddhi) : It is in the neck behind the throat-pit. Its sound is 'Hum'. Laughter and expression of gratefulness make it strong. It is called 'Vishuddhi Chakra'. Visuddhi means 'purifying'. It throws our the

poison of our body and retains the elixir of life. The elixir of life can be prepared within the body by the practice of sipping for about 30 minutes a day. You can drink the water that way or you can do it just orally. Its taste is like that of the oil of sesame, a bit sweet and astringent. It falls from the inner head on the center of the tongue and is dissolved within few seconds. Before it you may feel the poison coming out. Spit it out. Even if you cannot do it, it does not matter.

6. Sixth Chakra (Ajna) : It is located in the back-head, behind the eyebrow center. Its sound is 'Om'. Chanting of 'Om' should be done more than 40 minutes a day. Quality of this Chakra is balancing. Its main meditation is constant gazing (*Trataka*) on the wall, on the roof, candle light, in the sky, on any spot, in darkness. If it is practiced for a longer period, man can suffer from blindness because the image we see constantly is fixed in the eyes and wherever we see, we will not see the real object, that image will be seen.

7. Seventh Chakra (Sahasrara) : It is located just below the middle head. Its sound is humming (*Bhramari*).

   Begin Chakra - meditations with the sixth, seventh, fifth and fourth. Devote one month on each Chakra, then come to the third, second and first. For more details see my book 'Healing Hands'

Front portion of the Chakras

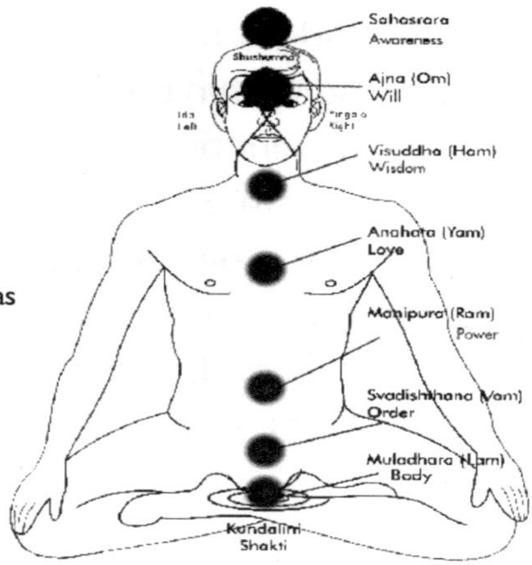

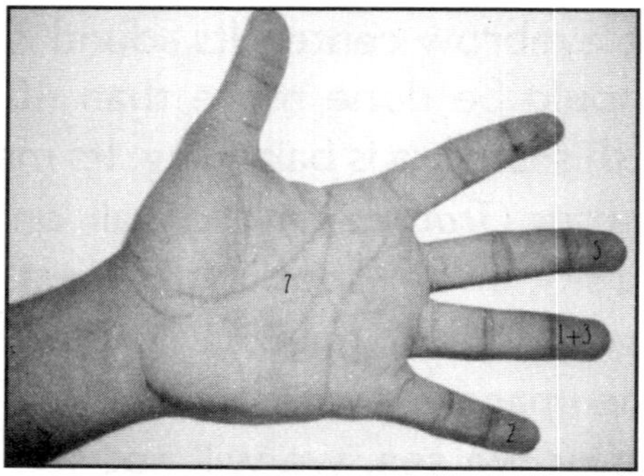

Chakras in the Hand
(Numbers stand for Chakras)

6. BALANCING CHAKRAS

Sometimes the Chakras, the energy wheels of our body are dislocated. To bring them in a line is called Chakra Balancing. If those are in a line their energy goes up and down and each Chakra is joined with the other. By Chakra meditations and by the Reikei, those are arranged in a line. Every Chakra comes up and down when it gets energy from the Universe. After the use of energy it stands still in its place in the backbone and throws the waste energy from its front portion. Our energy from the first to third Chakra goes up with a little effort. Similarly energy of fourth Chakra goes up to the seventh easily in a gradual process by normal efforts and vice versa. Link between the third and fourth Chakra is broken. I found that between these two Chakras is pancreas gland which supplies energy in all the parts of body by creating insulin for sugar. When I drew Reikei on pancreas, the third and fourth Chakras were easily joined. Fourth Chakra when joined with the third, sends upper energy to the earth and sends lower energy of the earth to the heaven. Here earthly energy is transformed. The electrical force becomes psychological and vice versa. So it is called Chakra balancing. It is between the three upper Chakras and three lower Chakras. Its symbol is six-pointed star. Two triangles fixed in each other. Lower triangle represents the lower energy going up and the upper represents heavenly energy coming down. Energy goes out by the pointed part of the triangle.

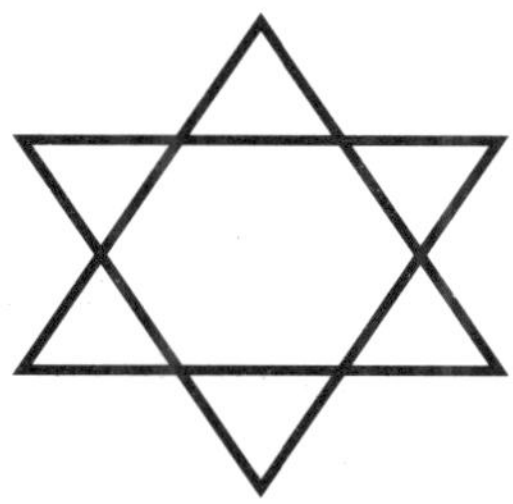

In Pyramids and temples all the negative energy gathers in the pointed upper part and is released in the space for purification. Fresh energy enters from below. Our rooms have four corners. Negative energy stays there as a block. It has no outlet. The fresh energy cannot enter as it does in the temples and pyramids.

7. BALANCING ENERGIES

Up and Down : In the Universe and human body, up and down currents of energy are working. Up going energy is called evolution or Kundalini and down coming energy is called devolution or Reikei. By meditations or sometimes without meditation one feels in the dream going up or down. Both currents of energy are required for keeping a man healthy. Lower energy makes our body strong and upper energy makes us mentally healthy. When we breathe in energy goes down and when we breathe out, it comes up. By meditations this process is magnified. Energy shows its movement through images. Such as rush of the traffic up and down, seeing the birds flying in the sky and a water fall coming on the earth.

Root Chakra is directly connected with the sixth Chakra. Energy given in the root Chakra, when its passage is clear, directly goes to the sixth and you will see the blue colour of sixth Chakra though you are meditating on the root Chakra and vice versa.

Right and Left: As we know that our one side is weak and one is strong if we see the birds flying towards the right side, it means our right side is strong. After efforts of balancing we will find that the birds have begun to flow on the left side also. Images of energies differ due to social atmosphere.

These energies are called 'Yin - Yang'. Both have potential to change in each other.

Front and Back : Energy working over our front side is concerned with our worldly activities. By meditations one comes to know that energy goes deep up to the backbone. Energy working in the backside supports our spiritual life. This energy can be activated if we walk backwards. It is dangerous if we stumble and fall down. For this purpose chose a big ground and have some attendant with you. This energy rises from the root Chakra of our foot heels and goes up to the front head. The movement of energy in the root Chakra is serpentine. Up to the third Chakra it jumps like a frog and from fourth Chakra it flies like a bird. In the backside the movement is liner.

In and Out: In our worldly life energy goes out and we know outward things. Purpose of Yoga is to make the movement of energy inward. Then we will know what is within our body. For this understanding we can practice certain exercises.

1. Stand and shake your hands quickly for 5 minutes. Stop suddenly. You will see the vibrations in the hands, energy coming in or going out.

2. Clap for 5 minutes and stop suddenly.

3. Choose a big ground and run as fast as you can, stop suddenly. You will see the process of running still going on. That is your vital aura. The first layer of energy on your body.

These are the inner experiences. You will enjoy daily new experiences. When the energy goes inward we feel fresh and cheerful. So our energy should work like an inverter. It should move in and out as required. We are habituated to drain our energy outside, by to much speaking, hearing, seeing and thinking. This is why we feel tired. Meditation means the energy should work inside our body, which keeps us always young. Function of 6th chakra is that of balancing, but it is disturbed by our disordered life. People, other than hindus, who will not accept the theory of Lord Krishna, should attribute it to 6th chakra.

8. BALANCING & PSYCHOLOGY

Pingala energy channel allows the right nose to breathe more and employs the person for working more mechanically. The persons who are busy too much or over active, they are workaholic. If they do not find any activity they are full of tension and restlessness. They talk too much or eat again and again. This is due to *Pingala*. On the other hand some persons are lazy, slow, not interested in over activity, want rest and sleep - that is due to *ida* channel of energy. It allows the left nose to flow more. By balancing the breath, we can balance our psychology. At the time of work we work carefully and at the time of rest we rest regularly. These energy channels go touching each Chakra. If Chakra is powerful, these channels spread the Chakra's energy in the body. If any Chakra is weak, the energy channels will not work. Every Chakra has its own psychology. It is difficult to understand for the common man that how these channels work. This is why the nature differs from man to man. Nowadays people are *Pingala* troubled. Everyman wants to rise in logical and mechanical intelligence.

INDEX

PART III

Spiritual Sun-Rise

1. LIFE OF A YOGI

Yogi should keep alone, 'Far From the Maddening Crowd'. Gita says a Yogi should avoid the crowd. When enlightened, he should be active to guide the other people though he has nothing to do for himself like Lord Krishna. There is no definite definition of a Yogi. He should lead a life as suited to him. There are all types of Yogis. Janaka was a king, Lord Buddha and Lord Mahavira renounced their kingdom, Kabir was a householder and earned his livelihood by weaving, Guru Nanakdev gave the responsibility of his family to his elder sister and left the home, saint Ravidas was a shoemaker and Mirabai who belonged to a royal family accepted him as her Guru. Yogi should live in a moderate climate. All his life should be moderate.

2. TRUTH AND SIMPLICITY

Truth is the basic element which supports the life of divinity. The Upanishads say, the path of divinity is full of truthfulness. This fact applies only in the life of divinity, on the way of spirituality, not in worldly life. People misunderstood it because they are not treading the path, which is less traveled but they are on the path of material life. If truth fails people say it will win in the end. But it happens rarely. Then people ask what is utility of truth. About this situation Shri Aurobindo says "Reward of virtue is not always material pleasure. Reward of virtue is to grow more in Love Light Divinity". Another author says "Reward of virtue is not always material pleasure, nor punishment is the result of sin". Good begets good, evil evil. Materially seen there is a loss or gain but psychologically truth gives happiness at once and fearlessness forever, while falsehood and crookedness stamp us with fear and inferiority and inner degradation.

By truth there is a smooth flow of energy in body while falsehood (means the suppression of truth) hinders the flow of energy, creates energy block and in turn clots which result in diseases.

3. SELF RESPECT

Self-respect, aspiration, honesty, sense of duty, gratitude, energy exchange and service, patience are spiritual qualities. In our country we are interested to rise above others to dominate and keep them suppressed. This sense of projecting ego and superiority at once changes into inferiority when we fail to do so, because energy moves to the opposite pole, from one extreme to the another. Self-respect is something between, always keeps us balanced even in adverse circumstances, we do not feel degraded and we do not suffer from ego in prosperity. We should fulfil our needs easily, should not try to be very rich even by honesty. Because accumulation of wealth in hands of few persons creates imbalance in society. The others are deprived of the work and earning. There should be no competition in any sphere. Everybody should work according to his ability and limits. Everyone should be respected.

4. UPANISHADS, TANTRA & YOGA

In Upanishads there are some methods of meditations and spiritual experiences. Those are very minor and incomplete. For example in Kathopanishad, Master Yama says to Nachiketa that chanting of 'Om' is all and there is no need of doing anything else. Chanting of 'Om' is only a meditation of sixth Chakra. Every Chakra has its own sound (*Bija Mantra*) to be chanted. All Chakras should be attended for one month respectively. We should begin by the sixth Chakra. Upanishads and Yoga books describe the vision of light as a major experience. But it is minor. Beyond it are the experiences of smell, taste, touch and sound.

Similarly in Taittiriya Upanishad there is a description of five Sheaths (*Panchakosha* - Aura). By reading Upanishad we come to know that these auras are within the body. Actually these auras are out of the body and their number is four, not five. Those can be photographed. Yoga books do not refer to Upanishads or Tantra books. Teachings of Tantra are also useful in spiritual growth. Animals are below morality, man is moral and angels are above morality because they have no physical birth. So they have no relation of a mother, sister or a daughter with females. They have only the partners as females. Tantras do not care for morality as the movie artists So Tantras were defamed and boycotted by the society. Where there is morality, hypocrisy prevails. In the history of England, there was a puritan movement, the puritans were highly moralistic. Most of them became hypocrites and were mocked at like Malvolio in the play of Shakespeare 'Twelfth Night'.

5. YOGA AS A HOBBY
(Karma Yoga, Nishkama Karma Yoga)

Main teaching of Gita is that our action should be based on our hobbies. It should be a joy in itself. Make it your profession and earning livelihood should be its by-product. It is akin to Yoga because it keeps our mind peaceful even in the adverse circumstances. It is also called '*Sahaja Karma*' (inborn). We can take interest only in the action which is our hobby. The vice versa will not do. It is also called '*Swa Dharma*' (Self - religion - Self nature). Human nature is divided into four classes in the world.

1. The persons who are interested in learning, teaching, preaching and meditations - they are called *Brahmins*.

2. Those wh are interested in governing, saving the nation, fighting and maintaining the law and order - they are called *Kshatriyas*.

3. Those who are interested in business with a sense of service to society - they are *Vaisyas*.

4. Those who are interested in labor, animal husbandry and agriculture.

The persons who stick to their nature give excellent services to society. Brahmins are advised to be vegetarians. If so, an enlightened person is born in their family in the fourteenth generation because their blood goes on becoming thin and fine. Gita says it is better to die in one's own *dharma* than to accept other *dharma*. Here *dharma* does not mean Hindu, Muslim or Christian, it is the nature of the man.

6. YOGA NIDRA (YOGA SLEEP)

In Hatha Yoga, there is a technique called 'Yoga Nidra' where man falls asleep. Purpose of Yoga should be to achieve awareness which is far superior and refreshing than the sleep.

People when feel boredom, begin to sleep. Just as in chanting mantras, hearing any sermon which is not appealing to them. That kind of sleep is not harmful but that is not helpful either in the spiritual growth. If one goes deep in the sleep his body becomes forzen and he can go into comma. In Raj yoga our parts of body melt and become so light that we feel as if we have lost the part.

7. WALKING AS YOGA

According to Shri Aurobindo "all life is a secret Yoga". Any activity can be made meditation. By Yoga I mean some inner experience which gives awareness. For this purpose go for a walk alone or if you are attended by your friends tell them to keep silent. While walking be aware of your feet - placing and taking up one by one. You will see that thinking stops, we think day and night and drain our energy. You will see that your nerves from feet are attached up to head and hemispheres work likewise. Maintain this awareness even in other activities as - breathing, actions, emotions, happenings of the world. This 'Vipashyana' (witnessing) meditation was proposed by Lord Buddha. So long as you are not balanced, walk according to the methods- as walking side ways or clock-wise as you need. When you are balanced then walk straight keeping your head in front. Do not gaze right or left.

8. TRAVELING AS YOGA

Traveling everyday and staying in any village only for one day is also a good meditation, though not possible nowadays. When we stay anywhere permanently, our contacts with so many persons are developed, which reduces us to live in the past and future. If anybody meets, we know him already, so he does. We see, talk and behave with our past experience and imagine about future relations. We are deprived of the present moment. Life is always in the present. Past is dead, future is unborn. When we go to a new place and meet a new person, we are in present and we cannot think of any past as we do not know him already.

" Thus yesterday, today, tomorrow come,
They hustle one another and they pass.
All our hustling morrows only make
The smooth today of God."

- Theocritus

Present moment is thoughtless - awareness - a meditation. We see the things as new, as was in childhood (Read the poem of William Wordsworth - 'An Ode' - Early Recollections from Childhood). The world seems as appareled in a celestial light.

Amongst the Indian Saints Guru Nanakdev was widely traveled. He walked on foot. Born in Punjab 500 years ago, he went up to Himalayas in the north, went to Assam in the east, went to Srilanka in the south and went to Mecca in Soudi Arabia. He was attended by two devotees Bala and Mardana. Guru Nanak was a poet. He wrote religious songs in the praise of God and his creation. Mardana was a musician who used to sing. Wherever Guru Nanakdev went, people came to know about his spiritual achievements. He wrote a book "*Pran Sanghly*" to teach Yoga to the king of Srilanka. This book deals with the Chakra healing and breathing exercises. In ancient times Srilanka was called Singhal Dweep means Singhal Island.

Pran means the book of Yoga written for the King of Singhal Dweep. He describes Chakras as lotus and Mahal (Palace). There is reference of *Ida, Pingala* and *Sushumna* energy channels also. He passed last days of his life in the Kartarpur town in Punjab.

Jain saints maintain this tradition today by walking on foot. Nowadays political leaders travel by plane to all the countries. That is not Yoga, because their programme is planned and they work by memory. They are not in contact with nature.

9. YOGA & BHOGA

Nowadays Yoga is meant for *Roga* (disease). A healthy man will say "I need no Yoga". Late Kaka Hathrasi (uncle who lives in Hathras town) wrote a book in Hindi language 'Yoga and Bhoga'. It is a humourous book. *Bhoga* means physical enjoyments. For me this book is serio-comic. This book is inspired by the teachings of Osho. Reikei Masters of Europe, Sigmund Freud, Tantra books, Osho recommend to express emotions because suppression is a mental disease. Moreover the energy of our lower Chakras (second Chakra is the Chakra of enjoyment) comes upward, we rise spiritually. Without enjoyments lower Chakras become dead and man becomes serious, sick, irritative and can never have any spiritual experiences, because the upper Chakras remain closed. Enjoyments should be taken as a necessity, not as the aim of life. If enjoyments are used as luxury, by the use of exciting drugs, those create fatal diseases.

Master Yama in Kathopanishad declares that there are two paths. One is of human mortals, the path of enjoyments.

Second is the path of gods, the path of meditations. We should choose the second path as it is good. These paths are not outward. Our Chakras contain both the paths. From 1st to 3rd Chakra, there is path of enjoyments and from 4th to 7th is the path of divine life. If we come from the lower path by living our life sincerely, our energy by itself goes to the fourth Chakra, the divine life. In Rug Veda hymn no. 10-85-45, it is said that a woman should give birth to ten children and her husband will be her eleventh son. It means, the sexual energy of a woman is transformed into divinity by giving birth to 10 children. (Nowadays there is no such need). She sees her husband with motherly affection. If we begin with the fourth Chakra and go up to seventh, the energy of devolution will bring us down to the first Chakra. Then again man will like to enjoy and people will say that he has fallen like '*Viswamitra*'.

10. RAJA YOGA

Raja Yoga means the Yoga for the king. A king cannot do something which is boring. He wants everything joyful. Hath Yoga is technical. In it we handle our body as a machine. Raja Yoga is creative. In it we love our life, our body, society and express our emotions by dancing and singing. These activities also lead to meditation, if clearly understood and properly done. Raja Yoga is a celebration, not an entertainment. Dancing, singing and playing by oneself is a celebration. And seeing a dance, or hearing a song is entertainment. Celebration is a complete action and we get rid of it after a few days. It makes no energy block. But in entertainment we cannot get rid of it for the whole life because by seeing only our energy blocks are not dissolved. But society does not allow for the celebration. It allows the entertainment.

You may ask that the movie artists dance and sing all their life. Can they be enlightened? The answer is 'No!'. Their dancing and singing is not a celebration for themselves but a profession for the others. There is 'Nataraj Meditation' of Osho. Here you have to dance for 40 minutes, then lie down for 20 minutes. For this purpose you need not learn a dance. Because the learnt dance will keep you on the level of memory and you can never get awareness. When we dance without learning, the suppressed waves of energy find their outlet and our dance becomes spontaneous. I have realised when we are dancing in a thoughtless position, our movement seems very beautiful to us. But when the thoughts begin, our movements seem very ugly.

Tansen was a famous singer in the court of Akbar. He sang for Akbar and his courtiers. Singing was his business. His Guru was saint Haridas, who lived in a forest. He used to sing for his own joy. Tansen was having all the knowledge of his Guru. Still Tansen is called a singer and Haridas is called a saint. It means the singing of Haridas was a celebration while singing of Tansen was a profession.

Human love is prohibited in society. So it found outlet in the form of love for God. Urdu poetry describes that God is at once forgotten when we think of our lover. Devotional poetry describes all types of human relationships with God. For example - He is a Master, son, father, brother, husband and even enemy. Ravan was devoted to Lord Ramachandra as an enemy. Sufi poets say that man loves his wife more than anybody in the world. So they accept God as their wife. It is all ignorance.

11. LOVE - BALANCING FACTOR

Up till now, love has been a mystery. It happens by itself, makes us calm and peaceful filled with the sense of wonder. It makes the hell a heaven. It is a rare happening. I think the love happens when the energies of man and woman are balanced. If a man having 60% male energy meets by chance a woman having 60% female energy, they will fall in love because both are balanced as a pair. Remaing 40% female of the man will join the 40% male energy of the women. Their energies are identified with each other, though the bodies are separate. Energies migrate through their eyes into their bodies. If some meter is invented to measure the male and female energies, love will be logical and a common incident. Marriages based on it will never need divorce. This will lead humanity to divinity. Nowadays what we call love is based on physical needs. Male and female energies can be measured by the vibrations of the hemispheres and the parts of the body of right and left.

In Hatha Yoga Vajrouli Mudra is a physical effort of balancing male and female energies. The same purpose is achieved by Osho's theory of love. In the communion of male and female our energies migrate in each other. If female energy dominates, male thinks that he has become female and vice versa. In the balance both lose their sense of sex and the question arises 'Who am I?'. God is neither male or female. So is the case with the enlightened persons. In our both sides of body there are male and female energies. We can join them by meditations without any partner. It is difficult but not impossible.

In 'Balancing Mudra' the same purpose is achieved. Both partners should sit face to face and join their fingertips and thumbs with both hands.

12. YOGA NIGHTS

"Yogi awakes in the night when the common man sleeps and a Yogi sleeps in the day when a common man is awake and works"

Gita - 2/69

Commentators of Gita explain that night means ignorance, not the real night. Here it means literally the night only. Because the implied meaning is used in literature, where the author cannot express his thoughts freely due to social customs. But in the books of history, physics, philosophy - there is nothing to hide. So whatever is written is really meant. I have realised, though we practice meditations in the day but the result occurs in the night.

Our first three Chakras receive energy from the stars in the daytime. By their energy we conduct our worldly affairs. I.

Root Chakra receives energy from the earth from 6.00 AM to 7.00 AM

2. Second Chakra receives energy from the moon from 7.00 AM to 1.30 PM

3. Third Chakra receives energy from the Sun from 1.30 PM to 8.00 PM

Our divine life begins with the fourth Chakra.

4. Fourth Chakra receives energy from Venus from 8.00 PM to 2.30 AM

5. Fifth Chakra receives energy from Mercury from 2.30 AM to 3.40 AM

6. Sixth Chakra receives energy from Jupiter
from 3.40 AM to 4.50 AM

7. Seventh Chakra receives energy from heaven
from 4.50 AM to 6.00 AM

If we are asleep, activity of the receiving energy by the Chakras becomes dull. For spiritual progress it is better to awake in the night and sleep in the day. You may ask that the watchman, the thief and some other persons on duty like drivers, Railway Station Masters awake at night, no spiritual progress is seen in their life. They must be gaining something spiritual of which they are not aware. But a Yogi who intentionally awakes in the night and practices meditations grows spiritually without any doubt.

If it is not possible for waking the whole night, you go to sleep at 9.00pm and wake at 12.00am. Even if it is not possible then leave it. Meditation should be a joy, not a tension.

13. MEDITATIONS

Patanjali in his 'Yog Darsan' chapter2 aphorism no. 54 defines the word 'Pratyaahaar' as "when the senses come in contact with their objects those behave like the mind". It means mind feels joys and sorrows through the senses and our enrgy goes out. It happens in our daily life. It is 'Aahaar'. Pratyaahaar contains 2 words 'Prati' and 'Aahaar'. 'Prati' means 'opposite' - 'reverse' and 'Aahaar' means 'diet' - 'objects of senses'. These objects are outward. If we can make our energy incoming, the objects of the senses will be found within as in the dream. So 'Pratyaahaar' means make your outgoing energy coming inward.

Osho defines meditation as 'quick activity and sudden stop'. In this way our outgoing energy becomes at once inward and we feel fresh, not tired. As we feel after exercises or some laborious work. This is the best form of 'Pratyaahaar'. Osho gives such type of activities as 'Dynamic Meditation' and 'Whirling'. This is the first step to the meditation, not meditation in itself. In the period of stop watch your breath. If you are breathing by the left or right nostril, you are imbalanced. Only half of your body is filled with energy by the side you breath, that energy overflows towards the other side and you feel that whole body has melted (became light). This is 'half body experience'. Osho's meditations need balance. George Gurdjieff also taught such 'stop exercises'.

Osho's meditations like 'Mystic Rose', 'Kundalini' and 'Nataraj' etc., remove energy blocks by catharsis those need no balance because an awareness is created. Imbalance ends in emptiness. These meditations should be classified separately and should be given some other name.

BALANCED BREATH (SAMA SHWASA)

There is a minute difference between the normal breathing by both nostrils and the balanced breathing. Normal breathing by both nostrils is due to tension and balanced breathing of *Sushumna* energy channel begins when the working of *Ida* and *Pingala* stops. In this breathing you will feel that you are not breathing at all. Breath becomes very thin. Generally this happens at the time of sunset and sunrise for three minutes for everybody if his life is peaceful. During this breathing body becomes very light and mind becomes calm. You will not like to eat or drink or to go somewhere or to talk to somebody. And you should not do these things with effort. Only sit in your room peacefully and watch the condition. For the meditators it may start at anytime and last for anytime. If *Sushumna* works for 15 days it opens the gateway to spirituality.

In any meditation don't be satisfied with the mental peace. Watch your breath whether it is balanced or one-sided. If it is one-sided, try to balance it.

14. KUNDALINI & REIKEI

When the flow of water is blocked by a rock in the river or the sea, it turns back and begins to move in a circle. Similarly our energy of past lives is blocked in our root Chakra and turns round. '*Kundal*' means a round, a circle. '*Kundalini*' means coiled energy. Here the blockage is 'fear' (lack of freedom by society) and the fear of the snake. In the past lives man has lived in the forests. So the fear of snake is almost inborn. So this energy is identified with the snake and its symbol is coiled snake. Movement of *Ida* and *Pingala* channels up to the sixth Chakra is serpentine but those are not snakes in our body. The fear of snakes dominates the meditator for a few years and diminishes when he sees a lion or any other wild animal like a bear or an elephant. As it is the energy of our past animal life, it is devilish, aggressive, violent. Its base is sex. Its seat is root Chakra. It is an evolutionary force, ready to go up. Hatha Yoga proposes physical exercises for awakening *Kundalini*. If it is released, man will behave like an animal and even he can go mad. To avoid this, it is suggested that we should begin by the sixth Chakra and we should also activate other Chakras to make the way for *Kundalini* to go up. Man is advised to practice

Hatha Yoga in the presence of Guru, which is not possible for everybody nowadays.

The better substitute of *Kundalini* is Reikei, which is quite opposite of *Kundalini*. It is loving, divine, blessed, peaceful energy of devolution, means coming down from heaven in our seventh Chakra and going down to the feet. There is no danger in it. If it is overdosed, either it stops or it flows to the other part of the body, because it is an intelligent energy. From seventh Chakra it comes to the fourth Chakra by itself. Our hands are motor organs of the fourth Chakra. So wherever we put our reikei hands reikei goes on that part and clears the negative energy and the blocks and gives energy in the body. Fourth Chakra is the seat of love. So the base of reikei is love. Lack of love turns in fear. The more we are loved the more we are fearless. If you cannot find others' love, you can love yourself by drawing reikei. Reikei is available in abundance, everywhere, every time. Man is born by love, lives by love, dies without love. He is ready to face the death for the sake of love. In reikei, initiation is required by the reikei Master. You should respect the reikei Master as your father or a saint but you need not stick to him forever. You may seek his guidance time to time. *Kundalini* activates our energy-blocks. When all the energy-blocks are activated, Yogi has to assume many forms to exhaust all blocks. This is strugglesome and unnecessary. On the other hand reikei goes on dissolving the blocks. When all the blocks are dissolved, man is enlightened. Symbol of reikei is healing hands and brilliant white light with a little blue tinge. Reikei guides life and we can proceed with confidence.

Reikei guides by the images of symbols. When I proposed this method of balancing, I wanted that somebody should confirm it. But I could not find somebody. In the practice of reikei I saw a lighted matchstick. After two or three days again I saw the lighted matchstick. I thought over its meaning and found that its meaning is, beginning is correct. Before cooking food, we light a matchstick. Whenever you undertake any action, you must think over about its balance.

← Proposed Reikei Symbol

Popular Kundalini Symbol →

15. ANGELS

Imbalance is a part of duality. This duality goes up to the divine life of angels because they have their opposite- devils and evil spirits. Imbalanced person if normally healthy and imbalance is normal and if he is 100% honest and full of love for everybody having a sense of service, goes to the life of an angel through the meditations of fourth Chakra. Similarly dishonest person, badly devoted to the life of enjoyments and blind towards his bad qualities becomes a devil. Angels and devils live for thousands of years until their hunger for joys is exhausted. Because in the human life there are many limits, one cannot enjoy fully. They are always young. Angels come once again in human life for meditations to achieve the final goal of *Moksha*. Even before they visit the earth for reformation.

"May we enjoy the company of angels" - veda

Man is a link between the animals and gods in the evolutionary process. As man has broken connections with the animals so has done with the gods. Man has come from the animal life and his destiny is god and further to be a Buddha. There are such currents of energy in his chakras.

Vedic rituals and prayers are all for calling the gods. Call compels an answer. Gods do come and exchange energies with human beings, as we do with the animals. It is not difficult to call gods. After second degree reikei you draw the distant symbol along with others, give reikei for three months, the god will some day come to you. For this purpose you should know the name of god. Ancient gods have left their bodies and entered once in human body and attained moksha by meditations.

Such gods will never come back. Some other gods may come, seeing your sincerity. Man is accompanied by gods and devils. If he is cent percent honest, gods accept him devils leave him for ever and vice versa. In reikei practice and initiations gods, spiritual guides, ascended masters take part. They correct our mistakes, and guide through images. Invoke those gods and you will feel their presence someday. They come at once by astral traveling.

There are hidden forces behind life. When we take meals gods or devils are present. Smell of the food is sufficient for them. The gods are present between 10AM to 11 AM. and 6PM to 7 PM. and the devils between 1PM to 3 PM. and 10PM to 12 midnight. In India gods have abandoned us since we take our food at the time of devils.

Qualities of gods are like those of human beings. Some are warriors, some are engineers, some are doctors etc. In Faith - Healing the healer invokes God and requests Him to send a healing angel for the patient. The angel comes and stays with the patient until he recovers his health. If a patient is near to death, the angel will not come. Devils are opposite of gods, they are full of negative energies for enjoyments at any cost. They are cruel, selfish, and violent and ugly. Their aura is muddy. They have no halo. At the end they surrender to the enlightened persons and enter divinity. Angels live under the guidance of enlightened persons.

16. MOKSHA
(The Blissful Seat)

There is a life beyond the stars
There is a life that knows no bars.

Mooch means to get rid of. *Moksha* means getting rid of all sorrows, troubles and worries. People are very unhappy. So this definition appeals to them and the word *Moksha* became popular. We live in the world of dualities. Joys and sorrows are connected with each other. Actually *Moksha* is a combination of both opposites. Joys and sorrows are mixed tegether and turn into Delight, a Bliss. Everything seems useful. Sorrows take us in the deep. If there are no sorrows in the world, our happiness will be shallow like that of a child.

A happy or sorrowful person is not always happy or sorrowful. There are certain moments when he feels at ease. This happens when we are partially balanced. By practice of meditations we enter a temporary samadhi (ecstasy). Adhi means mental troubles, diseases & energy blocks. Sama means made equal like mathematical equations. Joys and sorrows are equalized. We enter in the sound sleep in the same state but we know after waking that we were in the state of Bliss .

Though Lord Buddha was of the opinion according to *Sankhya* philosophy that his sorrows can be uprooted forever. But he was enlightened by the balancing of joys and sorrows. He enjoyed as a price and after renouncing the kingdom invited sorrows.

Moksha is a completely balanced state. A complete freedom. This is the state of enlightenment. This is the purpose of evolution. This is the destiny of every man. Someday man will be enlightened. His life of an angel and the enlightened person is standing behind him as a young man is standing behind a child and an old man is standing behind the young man. At the time of death, we are forcibly dragged to leave the body. But at the time of entering the sphere of angels, we leave body happily as if we have used it fully.

Whenever we meet some abnormal circumstances we are always aware about the outward result. If we watch within we will see a sense of wonder - a deep peace, a silence. It changes our psychology and breath. It creates a balance. We are such a customer who goes to the bank to draw some amount and is refused because he has no such balance for the desired withdrawal. If he draws the amount within his balance he will never be refused. In the bank we have to keep some balance for the future transaction. similarly our desires are kept in our subconscious mind for the future birth. If we close the account we need not go to the bank in future. Similarly when our desires are balanced we need not take any birth again. We go to the seat of eternal bliss.

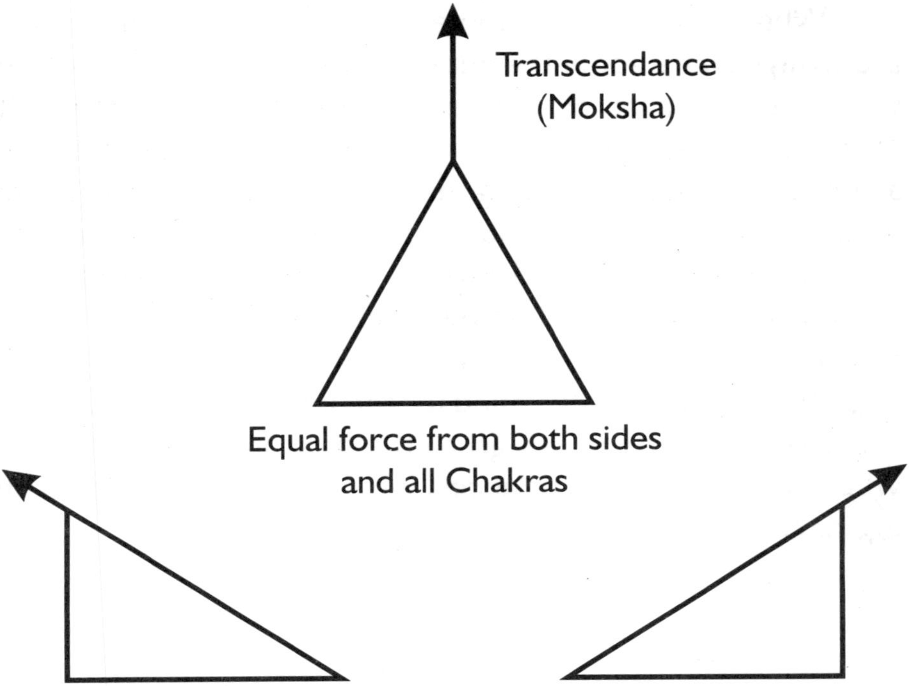

Right suppressed
by the Left

Left suppressed
by the Right

My Personal Growth of Balance

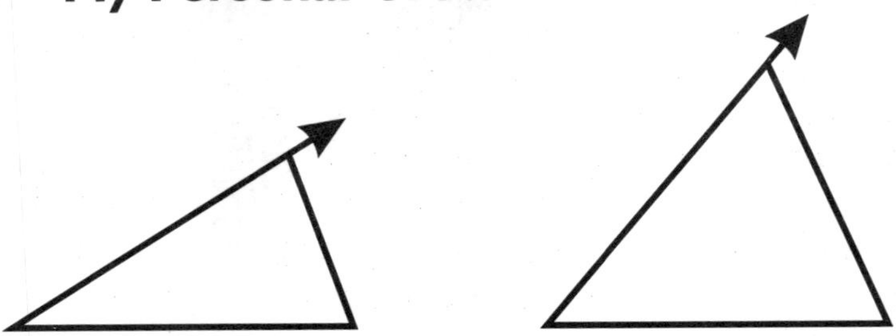

Left suppressed
by the Right
(Heart & Lung
suppressed)
Age : 65 years

Balance grew up to
shoulders
(Heart & Lung saved)
after 8 years of effort
for balance.
Age : 73 years

Proposed Training of Global Yoga :

1. Part of the this book is a Diploma Course.
2. Part is Degree Course.
3. Part is Yoga - Director Course.

"HEALING HANDS"

A book by the same author, it deals mainly with reikei and other allied subjects. There is a researchful and practical matter in this book. There is a detailed description of energy blocks, Chakras and their meditations. Philosophical theories are clearly understood. There is a smooth flow in the arrangement of topics. Reikei signals is a new topic in it based on personal experience. The author has given practical shape to certain Veda Mantras such as 'white light imagination' and 'dark energy imagination' are shown as meditation. This book is mainly a practical explanation of a *mantra* in Atharva Veda (4-13-6) about the healing power of touch.

Opinion

Amarjit Oberoi
Retired DANICS officer
Govt. of Delhi,
463, Nimri Colony,
Near Ashok Vihar Phase IV,
Delhi-110052

I have known Swami Nigmanand Ji for a decade. He is an ardent practitioner of Yoga and meditation techniques. He has made a lot of original research in this field. He has also learnt Reiki upto the Master Level and has well incorporated Reiki with other techniques. He has already got published some books on these subjects.

His latest book, 'Global Yoga' is a revoloutionary one. In the first chapter of his book named 'Need for Balance', he has explained the need for balancing the right and left hemispheres and sides of the body to achieve a healthy body and mind.

This is the solid base on which the whole structure of the book stands. I have read this book more than once, and found it really useful as a preliminary knowledge before practising any exercises–Yogic or otherwise. It is a 'must read' book for practitioners and teachers of Yogic exercises. I have myself started practising some of these balancing exercises and feel the increase in energy level.

I hope this book will soon be popular among the people who are interested in maintaining healthy body and mind. By following the techniques taught by Swami*ji*, everyone will be greatly benefitted, specially the future generations.

Amarjit Oberoi
Author's Reiki Master